Arabic Writing
and
Arab Libraries

S. M. Imamuddin

Ta Ha Publishers
68a, Delancey Street, London NW1 7RY. U.K.

British Library Cataloguing in Publication Data
Imamuddin, S. M.
Hispano-Arab libraries.
1. Islamic libraries — History
2. Libraries — Spain — History
3. Manuscript, Arabic — Spain — Catalogs
I. Title

027.6'7   Z675.1

ISBN 0-907461-29-8

First Printed 1983

Filmset, printed and bound in Great Britain for Ta Ha Publishers, 68a Delancey Street, London, NW1 7RY. By Delux Printing Press London.

Contents

PREFACE

This short memoir belongs to the series of papers and small books written so far on the subjects by the present writer. Before going to Spain on Study Leave, in September 1953, he had started taking classes on Islamic calligraphy and Numismatics with the Final year M. A. Students in his own department at the University of Dacca and on his return, in June 1956, he was induced to teach the same subject as an honary teacher in the Library Science department newly established under the chairmanship of his highly esteemed friend Mr. M. S. Khan, the then Librarian of the Dacca University. This gave the present author an opportunity to have a better idea of the subject under review here and accordingly he published two papers consecutively on Muslim Libraries in Spain in the *Journal of Pakistan Historical Society,* Karachi, 1959, which later appeared as Memoir under the title *Hispano – Arab Libraries,* Karachi, 1960. He also published another article on *Paper Manufacture in Muslim Spain* in the monthly Bulletin of Dacca University Library, Vol I, No. 8, August 1958, edited by the same librarian.

Meanwhile the author continued to collect materials on the subjects and published recently a paper on Islamic Calligraphy and read another one, the *Impact of 'Arabo-Persian Calligraphy'*, in an International Seminar on Arts in Islamic Lands held at Farnham Castle (London). He also wrote a Memoir on *Some Leading Libraries of the Muslim World* with special reference to Indo-Muslim Libraries which is still in the press of Islamic Foundation, Dacca. He published a note on *Arab Historiography* as an Introduction to his book *A Political History of the Muslims* Vol II, part I, in 1973.

The present author will feel amply rewarded if this small work succeeds in creating an interest in the students and readers. For all drawbacks in the text he himself is responsible and will try to remove them in future if pointed out by some learned reviewers.

37a, Stamford Road,   S. M. IMAMUDDIN
London N1,

August 8, 1982

INTRODUCTION

Prophet Muhammad's secretariat functioned in its elementary form during his lifetime. The official transactions were registered by al-Mughirah b. Shu'ayb and Hasan b. Namir. Letters addressed to Kings and Chiefs were drafted by Zayd b. Thabit and sometimes by 'Abd Allah b. Al-Arqam. Under the first caliph Abu Bakr, Hadrat 'Ali was placed in charge of correspondence besides supervising the captives of war. Hadrat 'Umar established a Diwan on his accession to the *Khilafat* to register the names of the recepients of pensions and to deal with correspondence as well as finance.

To handle the official letters, mandates, diplomas and other state papers there was a board of correspondence of chancery office called *Diwan al-Rasalat* under the Umayyads and Abbasids and *Diwan al-Insha* under the Fatimids. Provincial revenue registers were maintained in Pahlavi in Mesopotamia and Persia, in Greek and Syriac, in Syria and, in Greek and Copt, in Egypt. The Arabicization work which has begun under the second Caliph 'Umar al-Faruq, was completed under the Great Umayyad Caliph 'Abd al-Malik. At the suggestion of Salib ibn 'Abd ab-Rahman, a Persian Mawla of Sijistan, 'Abd al-Malik ordered the keeping of records, accounts and correspondence relating to Government business in Arabic throughout the empire in and from 693 A.C., the year the first pure Arab gold dinars and silver dirhams were struck at Damascus with Islamic religious formulas. Even the papyrus produced in Egypt was stamped with the words, ('Say, He alone is God') in place of the former seal of the cross and Christian formula to the great annoyance of the Greeks when it was exported to their lands leading to the levy of duties on merchandise, the movement of which had been so long generally free between the 'Arab and Byzantine territories, and the strict vigilance was kept on postal (*barid*) service called 'the eyes and ears of the King'.

The *Surahs* (verses) of the Holy *Qur'an* were collected under the Chairmanship of Zayd b. Thabit during the Khilafat of Abu Bakr. These were re-edited under the third Caliph Hadrat 'Uthman based on the original copy of the *Qur'an* lying with the Prophet's wife

Hafsah follwed by the compilation of the Prophet's saying (*Hadith*) of which, according to the Sunni point of view, there appeared six reliable editions like Bukhari, Tirmidhi, Muslim, Mishkat etc under the early Abbasids. The Second Abbasid Abu Ja'far al-Mansur established a bureau of translations attended by scholars, scientists and linguists to discuss academic problems and translate books into Arabic Greek, Pahlavi and Sanskrit and it was further developed under the name of *Baytal-Hikmah* by the Abbasid Caliphs, Harun and Ma'mun, in the line of the Chinese Academy of Learning called *Han-Lin-Yaun* of Ming Huang and later a parallel institution grew up in Egypt under the sixth Fatimid Caliph al-Hakim bi-Ilah with the name *Daru'l Hikmah.*

Despite the early administrative, economical and social problems the Muslims had to find time for the development of Arabic letters by introducing *'Irab* system and simplifying the angular form of the Arabic letters and also of the language by writing books on grammar, rhetoric and prosody. The Arabs from the very beginning of Islam took a keen interest in the philosophy, subject and method of education and tried to solve their basic problems mutually by discussing them and writing books on education system. Arabic pedagogical literature is very rich, but most of the books on it are stil in manuscript forms and need attention of the scholars. For overall improvement of their knowledge the Muslims wrote books on history, especially *ghazwah* and *Tabaqat* forms, geography (routes and countries), astronomy, medicine, arboriculture, agriculture and other sciences. Madrasahs were founded with libraries attached to the Mosques which worked besides the prayer halls as the center of Muslim education and learning throughout the Muslim countries, as for example the Cordova Mosque Madrasah was then the Oxford University of the Umayyad Spain and al-Azhar of the Fatimids is still functioning as one of the highest seats of learning in Egypt. Madrasah, as a separate and independent institution, however, grew up later under the Abbasids, among which Nizamiyah and al-Mustas—ariyah of Baghdad topped the list. Under the Buwayhids the centre of learning shifted to Shiraz and under the petty dynasties and some powerful Sultans, other centres of learning came up in other towns and regions.

All these Mosque Madrasahs and institutions had their libraries beside the Imperial Libraries of the Umayyads, Abbasids and

Fatimids. The later Abbasid and Fatimid Caliphs of Iraq and Egypt and the Umayyad Caliph 'Abd al-Rahman III and al-Hakam II of Spain donated their personal collections to the central library growing rapidly in their capitals. Rare manuscripts were purchsed at high prices or copied in foreign lands by travellers and Caliph's agents. Native scholars were patronized and foreign ones were invited to assist them in the translation works and in the production of original writings.

It is pathetic, however, to note here that while Muslim libraries and Arabic manuscripts sustained irrepairable losses at the hands of the Christian rulers in Spain during and after the period of reconquesta, the Muslim libraries elsewhere suffered tremendously due to the jealousy of sects and schiism and political rivalry of Kings and Chiefs.

During the time of the Prophet *adim* (leather) and *'Asib* (palmleaf) were used for writing missionary letters. Pieces of camel's bones ('azam especially *aktaf*) were also used by the early Muslims but pot-sherds (*khazaf*), wooden tablets and flat white stones (*lakhaf*) were rarely used. The use of parchments called *raaq* or *jild* (finished leather), because of high price, was limited to the writing of documents and making of copies of the *Qur'an*. Papyrus called *Qirtas Misri* was another material for writing. It was made of a plant of the sedge family grown on the banks of the Nile from where it spread all over the world, but the last two materials for long writing were limited in quantity and being costly were beyond the means of the commoners. By the time of the Umayyads, the wide expansion of Islamic education and learning needed cheap materials in appreciable quantity for writing and translating books in large numbers and the need was fulfilled by the manufacture of paper in the 'Arab world and the interest taken by the calligraphists. The Arabs learnt the art of manufacturing paper from the Chinese in the early eighth century A.C., but the earliest manuscript written on paper are at Baghdad, dated 256H/870 A.C. and at Cairo, dated 265H/878-9 A.C. Criticizing the Berber merchants Maqdisi (*Kitab Ahsan al-Taqasim*) Leiden, 1906, p.239) writes in 985 A.C. that they carried their documents and the Holy *Qur'an* written on pieces of leather while Andalusion Muslims had already become experts in utilizing paper as writing material. In 947 A.C. the Byzantine ambassador came to the court of Hajib al-mansur at Cordova with a letter written in Greek upon skyblue paper. In the library of the Escorial near Madrid there are preserved a number of manuscripts in Arabic and Catalan written on cotton paper and dated as early as the 10th century A.C. The latest papyrus documents preserved in the Egyptian Khedivial and Vienna libraries are dated 319H/931 A.C. and 323H/935 A.C. respectively.

In the absence of the printing press and the modern devices of photo duplicating xerox, and other machines, the scribe was an obiquitous figure and he contributed largely to the art of 'Arabo-Persian calligraphy briefly reviewed in the text. The libraries also discussed therein shortly had a number of scribes on the permanent staff. To publishe their work in order to meet the increasing demand of the serious students and interested readers some authors also employed calligraphers. Their services were also required at flourishing bookshops. Some of these scribes were themselves calligraphists of eminence like Ibn Nadim, the author of al-*Fihrist*, and Yaqut, the famous geographer (d. 1128 A.C.).

Calligraphy occupies the central place in Islamic art pervading Islamic civilization but ignoring the cultural importance of the subject, western art historians have focussed far more on Islam's figural than on its calligraphic arts. The impact of Islamic calligraphy is remarkably noticed on the Muslim architecture, especially mosques and tombs, minor and industrial arts, miniature paintings and numismatics, a subject which needs separate treatment and readers may be referred to the present author's paper read in the First International Seminar on the Arts in Islamic Lands held at Farnham Castle not far from London on March 26-28, 1982, and to his other paper on Islamic Calligraphy published in the journal Asiatic Society of Bangladesh Dacca, 1981. Realizing the cultural importance of Islamic Calligraphy now interest is growing to hold exhibitors and conferences in Asia, Europe and America and to write papers and books on its different aspects. The present memoir is partly the result of the same interests. It will be commendable if the impact of Islamic Calligraphy is studied thoroughly from the artistic point of view in relation to other fine arts foccusing duly its impact on Muslim architecture, other fine arts and numismatics.

SECTION I

ARABIC WRITING

Palaeography:- Arabic writing which owed its origin to Syriac and spread throughout Arabia from Hirah or Anbar[1] might have remained confined in Arabia but for Islam whose wide expansion made it the language of the people in the surrounding countries and al-Maghrib (North Africa and Spain). It was Islam which helped it in overpowering the Syriac and Greek writings in Syria, Palestine and Mesopotamia, the Pahlavi script in Persia, Coptic in Egypt and Berber in North Africa and suppressed their growth and expansion for some centuries to come.

In their earliest stages Arabic consonant letters did not have dots and diacritical signs (*i'rab*), but after the spread of Islam when non-Arabs accepted Islam they felt difficulty in reciting their religious scriptures correctly with confidence which necessitated the introduction of short vowels and the writing of Arabic grammatical inflection *(I'rab)*. The newly founded cities of Basrah and Kufah by the second Caliph Hadrat 'Umar played their special roles in the development of Arabic script and grammar and in the growth of punctuation and *I'rab* system in which case the services of Abdu'l Aswad al-Du'ali (d. 688 A.C.) and Khalil ibn Ahmad will always be appreciated.

Besides the great similarity of the Arabic letters with the syriac and Hebrew writings in form and character their ancient numerical arrangement called *Abjad* is also the same. The discovery of a number of papyri inscriptions proves that their scripts do not differ essentially from the ordinary cursive script called *Naskh* by the Arabs.

The discovery of two inscriptions which are the earliest monuments of Arabic writing e.g. the trilingual (Greek, Syriac and Arabic) inscriptions of Zebed which dates from 512 A.C. and the bilingual (Greek and Arabic) inscription of Harran in the Lija dating from 568

A.C. shows a close resemblance to a number of inscriptions discovered from the Sinai ¡peninsula. The Siniatic inscription is written in Nabataean language, a dialect of Aramaic. The type of writing of these inscriptions is later than that of the other Nabataean inscriptions found scattered from Damascus to Madinah dating from the beginning of the Christian era. They represent the cursive writing used by the Nabataean in every day life especially in their capital Petra in the second and third centuries of Christian era. The cursive writing was developed earlier to the stiff angular script of the coins and inscriptions. It is too technical a subject to be discussed elaborately here. The earliest Arabic documents discovered so far bear a striking resemblance to the *Naskh* writing of modern Arabic. The next development in Arabic palaeography is the introduction of the stiff angular script called *Kufi*. Thus the views 'Naskhi writing is a development of the stiff angular script' held for long is not correct.

The Nabataean or Syriac cursive writing was further simplified and developed into the Arabic script towards the end of the fifth century of the Christian era. The present arrangement of the Arabic letters with strokes to join one with another dates back to the pre-Islamic period. The *Maghribi* writing which originated towards the second century of Hijrah era and differed from the oriental *(Mashriqi)* arrangement of the Arabic letters corresponds partly to the old Nabataean order and partly to the peculiar arrangement of the Arabic letters. Before the advent of Islam the cursive style of Arabic had already developed the fundamental characteristic of Arabic script namely the ligatures which joined one letter with the other.

To obviate the double insufficiency of the original alphabet e.g. to distinguish between letters of the same group but of different sound and to show with what vowel a letter was to be enounced *i'rab* signs, dots and short vowels had to be introduced. Setting aside the claim of the Arabs, that dots were invented by them to distinguish letter of similar form and shape, Moritz opines that following the model of the Syriac writing dots had been introduced before the advent of Islam although exact date of their introduction he could not determine and adds that dots were certainly used in the first century of Muslim era though not extensively as it was done later.²
Towards the end of the first and beginning of the second century one dot of ڧ (*qaf*) was placed in Egypt sometimes above and at other

10

times beneath the letter and in Palestine it was put below while ف (fe) was given no dot. In the second century ڧ was given one dot beneath the letter (ڢ) and later above it (ڣ) and thereupon ق (qaf) was given two dots. The Maghribi writing still retains the old punctuations of ق = ڢ (qaf) and ڧ = ڢ (fe).

Moritz claims that the short vowel signs (fathah = ـَ , Kasrah = ـِ and dammah = ـُ) were borrowed from the Syriac and they were indicated by putting one dot in the case of ا (a) above the letter, in the case of و (u) before the letter and in the case of ي (i) below the letter and the nunnation (تنوين = ـً , ـٍ and ـٌ) was expressed by doubling the dots. Abu'l Aswad al-Du'ali is credited, according to Ibn Khallikan, with the introduction of vowel signs:- fathah one dot above the letter (ـٔ), dammah a point before the letter (• —) and Kasrah, a point beneath the letter (ـٔ), which we still find in some of the old Kufic manuscripts of the Qur'an marked in red and sometimes blue. The diacritical signs were written with black ink and vowel points were used of different colour in the ancient manuscripts. Hughes[3], while making assessment of Ibn Khallikan's statements on the introduction of dots and vowel signs, tries to harmonise them by concluding that Abu'l Aswad ad-Du'ali invented simple vowel points (nuqqat), Nasr 'Asim introduced tanwin by following Abu'l Aswad and doubling points and Yahya ibn Ya'mar, who had acquired his knowledge of grammar from Abu'l Aswad al-Du'ali, completed the system by devising the i'jam, diacritical signs of the consonants. Later, points, as short vowel signs, were replaced with the shorter forms of ا , ي and و , the long vowels, fatahah Kasrah and dammah (ـَ , ـِ and ـُ) by Khalil ibn Ahmad, the founder of the Science of Arabic prosody and rhetoric. Thus the short vowels were derived from the weak consonants (long vowels) themselves. Towards the end of the 7th century A.C. the short vowels were used only with Kufic script in copying the Qur'an.

Calligraphy:- Viewing fine handwriting is a pleasure to the eye, joy to the heart and fragrance to the soul, because of the religious restrictions on the representation of living beings the early Muslims stimulated the art along decorative channels — specially in the realm of book production, in the art of copying and illuminating manuscripts, Islamic calligraphy may, therefore conveniently cliam a place among the greatest achievements of man's artistic activity. Of the

11

two elementary styles of Arabic script *viz naskhi* and *Kufi*, the cursive and angular, the latter was selected as the script of the government offices. In the beginning for about four centuries Arabic was used immensely in highly literary productions but gradually it gave way to artistic and decorative character. A number of manuscripts were written in different styles of Arabic writing and a number of monuments were decorated with Arabic inscriptions specially in Kufic characters. Because of its monumental character, the angular Kufic script drew the attention of artists so much that while achieving perfection in ornamental lines it lost its original purpose as the script of a language after about three centuries of its monopoly giving place to its rival the cursive script of the people. For ornamental purpose it was, however, used for two centuries more till it became obsolete.

The origin of the Kufic or the angular style of Arabic script is traced back to about one hundred years before the foundation of Kufah (17 H/638 A.C.) to which town it owes its name because of its development there. It was here that this style was used for official purpose. For the first two centuries of *Hijra* era it did not become a decorative style. A copy of the *Qur'an* dated 168H/784-5 A.C. is written in simple Kufic.

The cursive (*Naskhi*), Himyarite and monumental form of Arabic script, is derived from the Nabataean which is itself drawn from the *Phoenecian* of the 8th century B.C. Some Himyarite inscriptions adorned in conventional styles with animate and other objects and the Sabaean inscriptions decorated with ornamental design have come to light.[4] Because of the writing materials being hard they were written in angular form. The other more common form of writing was cursive which was developed into Arabic script before the angular Kufic style came into use and was written on soft material like papyrus and parchment. Historically Arabic is the youngest script of the world but it spread very widely along with Arab conquest and trade and became only second to Roman script in the world.

Coming into close contact with the Syriac when the cursive script was developed in the style of the Syriac, angular letter of Arabic writing came into being. The oblique and vertical lines are the main features of Kufic writing. By the end of the second century of *Hijra* era it reached its extreme angular character. By the middle of the 4th century of Hijra era the Kufic gave way to the *Naskhi* style. With the fall of the Fatimids who patronised the Kufic form of writing, it became obsolete. Intertwining and interlacing floral and geometrical forms of the Kufic evolved in the 5th and 6th centuries of the *Hijra*. From the very primitive stage Kufic possessed a vigorous decorative character. Vertically short its letters intensify by contrast the force of the originals in which length and weight are increased by the close crowding of the heavy loops.

Abu'l Aswan (d. 69H/688 A.C.), a disciple of Hadrat 'Ali, is credited with the improvement of the orthography of the *Qur'an*, introduction of vowel signs and diacritical marks. His system was followed for about a century. Then came Khalid b Yazid, who illuminated the *Qur'an* with gold and carved golden inscriptions on the Prophet's Mosque, Khalil ibn Ahmad (d. 170H/786-7 A.C.) the grammarian, and 'Ali ibn Kusai (182H/798 A.C.), the teacher of Ma'mun al-Rashid, further developed the Kufic style but it reached its excellence in the hand of Ibn Muqlah (338H/949-50 A.C.), the renowned court artist of al-Qahir lli'llah, the Abbasid Caliph. He invented five main styles which survived the Kufic and wrote a book on calligraphy in verse. The Persians had invented seven main styles of Pahlavi writing according to the subject matter of pre-Islamic days. Under Islam, they preferred *Kufi* in the beginning and *Naskhi* later. Dateable 10th century Kufic calligraphy is available from Persia. The Kufic forms were well adapted to the decorative style of the period.

For centuries *Kufi* and *Naskhi* were used side by side. The cursive (round curve) variety of the Arabic script which came to be known as *Naskhi* continued to be used for common purposes, in making correspondence and writing books, and developed unnoticed replacing the Kufic. Ultimately it came to be recognised as the script adopted by the government. Incorporating the orthographical improvements which had been worked out in the Kufic appeared fully developed with vowel marks, punctuations and diacritical signs. While Kufic developed in the lines of ornamental rhythm and decorative style it became a dead style for writing purposes, the *Naskhi* was developed in the lines of grace keeping the genuine features of the script and increasing the longevity. The calligraphists beautified the *Naskhi* script by changing the proportions of strokes and curves of its letters after the liking of the readers to secure better appreciation. They changed angles of the *Kufi* scripts into round curves and let strokes follow the natural sweep of the hand without interferring with the outlines of their anatomy and their orthography. They tried to express their emotion through the medium of linear rhythm making letters graceful.

Through gradual development of the *Naskhi* script, scores of new styles came in but only a few of them could survive the taste of the readers as they were products of fancy and did not evince the utility of art, a defect which also proved suicidal in the case of ornamental Kufic. Of its offshoots the *Gulzar*, the *Tughrah*, the *Ta'us* and the *Zulf-i-'Urus* were set apart for displaying the ingenuity and ornamental fancy. Throughout the course of the development of Arabic script, the tendency of the calligraphists had been to simplify the complicated and angular script to an easier and the more round one.

The *Naskh* representing the cursive Kufic style is softened to broader curves and freer sweeps. Its curves are neither perfectly round nor oval which is the characteristic of the *Nasta'liq*. Retaining slightly its angular origin, it holds a middle position between the Kufic and *Naskhi*. In the process of its development towards the round script, *Nasta'liq*, the *Naskhi* was marked distinctly by its offshoots, *Thulth* and *Riqa'*. It is mostly used by Arabic speaking people while *Nasta'liq* is peculiar to the Persian and the Urdu.

The *Maghribi*, the earliest variety of the *Naskhi*, is drawn directly from the Kufic of the second Century A.H. It was originally known as *Qairawani*, derived from Qayrawan, the Muslim Capital of *al-Maghrib*.[5] Algerian and Tunisian *maghribi* styles did not differ but the *Fasi* style was rounder than the Algerian variety of the *Naskh*. With the foundation of Qayrawan in 670 A.C. an intellectual centre was developed in the West. Under the patronage of Aghlabids of North Africa a Qairawani style of Arabic writing developed and under that of the Umayyads in Spain an Andalusian, the former being more stiff and the latter, round. The Maghribi style which is partly *naskhi* though more akin to Kufic preserves the punctuations of the second century Kufic writings as in the case of ف (fe) and ق (qaf) with one dot but difference in its position.

Angular script prevailed more in Persia and its surroundings than in the Arabic speaking countries and was more common than the *Naskh*. With the blending of the two scripts, *Kufic* and *Pahlavi*, the old

14

Persian script, there developed a new round style, *Ta'liq*, which was later under the impact of the *Naskh* gave birth to *Nasta'liq*. Although the latter was introduced much earlier, books were written in this style not before the 13th Century A.C. Persian verses were composed and marginal commentaries and interlinear translations of the Quranic verses were made in this style. Main contents of the *Qur'an* were never written then in the *Nasta'liq*, but always in *Naskh*. Its strokes are long and bluntly pointed. They flow easily straight or horizontally but they never descend slantlingly as they do in *Thulth, Riqa', Raihan, Divani* and *Shikastah*. It has been rightly observed by a European orientalist "while *Haskh* is substantial, equable and assured, and *Ta'liq* forceful, dominating, arbitrary, *Nasta'liq* is polished, elegant, easy and casual, the expression of a highly civilized sophisticated people."[6]

Under the Mamluks of Egypt there were current six official scripts as enumerated by Qalqashandi (8th Century A.H.) in his voluminous work:

a. *Al-Tumar al-Kamil,* written in several types and used in the official correspondence of the Sultans;
b. *Mukhtasar al-Tumar*, written in two variations *al-Muhaqqaq* and *al-Thulth*;
c. *Al-Thulth* has again two forms, *al-Thaqil* and *al-Khafif;*
d. *Al-Tawqi',* written in three forms *Tawqi', Badr al-Kamilah,* and *Walayat* — they are imperfect distortions of the *Nasta'liq* style;
e. *Al-Ghubar*, written in one form only; and
f. *Al-Riqa',*, written in three forms.

Under the Turks in the 13th Century A.H./19th Century A.C., there were used thirty forms of Arabic writing, out of these six were more prevalent:

a. *Divanih*, written in two forms, *Jali* and *Khafi*. The former bold letter was used by Imperial chancellery and the latter small form was used side-by-side with *Ta'liq;*
b. *Thulth*, used for ornamental purpose;
c. *Ta'liq*, round script, used for writing poetry only;
d. *Naskhi*, cursive, used for writing books especially scientific and religious works;
e. *Riqa'*, an official script of the Turks occasionally used in private

life;

f. *Ajazah*, rarely used.

Some of these important forms of writing need description to understand their nature and distinctive features.

Thulth is the ornamental variety of the *Naskh* style. It differs from the *Naskh* only in proportion of its curves and strokes which are about three times of the size of those of the *Naskhi* style. It is written in bold curves and wide swinging waves. In sweep it resembles the *Divani* style and also the *Shikastah*.

Riqa' is more ornamental than *Thulth*. It is very graceful and its strokes move like a creeping snake or the ripples of a stream.

Muhaqqaq is also a decorative style, the letters being thick and bold characters. In curves and strokes it is similar to another style of writing called *Raiyhani*, but bolder in characters. Its strokes are not slanting but break abruptly.

Divani, written diagonally from the top to the bottom of the page or vice-versa ascending eliptically. It is an offshoot of *Naskh*. In its intricate varieties here the letters run together rendering the reading difficult.

Zulf-i-'urus is a decorative style of the *Nasta'liq*. Its strokes are thick in the middle and end in straight points unlike *Thulth* without turning up in curve.

Ghubar is a very fine form of writing, the letters are small and appear like fleeing dust.

Mahi, Gulzar, and *Ta'us* are purely ornamental treatment of other styles and they are not styles themselves. They are not written but drawn in outline producing fish, flowers or birds like peacocks, and filled in with decorative lines with animals or flowers.

The *Larzah* is also not a style. It is written in such a way that the script appears to have been inscribed by a hand shaking with excitement.

Tughra owes its origin to the Turkish ruler, an official monogram composed of a fixed protocol. It is used as an amulet by the superstitious persons. A Quranic verse or a common prayer is drawn in *Tughra* style composing outlines of a bird or a tiger, or an elephant or other animals excepting unclean ones. Names of Allah, Muhammad (Prophet), Fatimah, 'Ali and other caliphs are also written in *Tughra* characters. It was also used for monumental inscriptions of which the striking one is in the *Masjid-i-Jami'*, Abarquh.

Shikastah is a broken form of *Nasta'liq* writing introduced during the Safavid period in the 16th century with a tendency of reverting to *Ta'liq*. The relation which *Divani* bears to Arabic *Naskh,* is born by *Shikastah* to the Persian *Nasta'liq*.

As it took a long time to write in *Nasta'liq, Khatt-i-Shafi'a* was invented for daily and rough use about the time when *Shikastah* writing was used in Mughal India. Both these writings were used mostly in the courts and offices. Because of the droppage of dots and the use of broken letters the reading of the *Shikastah* style is difficult. Among the best components of the *Shikastah* were *Shafi'a* (d. 1152/1739), Darvish 'Abd al Majid of Taliqan (d. 1206/1791) and his pupil Mirza Kujak of Isfahan and among other calligraphers of this style were Gulistana, Qa'im Muqam and Amin al-Dawlah. It was invented by Shamba or Shafi'a and perfected by the famous 'Ali Riza 'Abbasi, Darvish 'Abd al-Majid being the supreme master of this style.

Calligraphists:- The profession of a calligrapher was one of honour and dignity in Islam. Calligraphy has a subtle affinity with human and floral forms and possesses a remarkable adaptibility to pictorial rhythm. As an art calligraphy had become so important that professional artists, skilled men of arts and crafts, learnt and practised it in order to achieve success in their trades. The jeweller, the goldsmith, the copper and ironsmith, the seal engraver, the lapidary, the wood and stone engravers and the potters all tried to achieve efficiency in calligraphy and they often made themselves masters of several styles and wrought their wares with beautiful inscriptions. On aims and methods of scribes and calligraphers there was written *Kitab al-Kuttab* by Ibn Durustuya (258-347H/872-952 A.C.)

Scholars, kings and nobles all tried for the cultivation of calligraphy. The Muhaddith Ibn-al-Jawzi and Jawhari, the author of the *Sahah*, were great calligraphers. Wazir Abu Ja'far ibn 'Abbas, and *Andalusian*, was a great calligraphist. Safinah of Seville was unparalleled in the art of calligraphy. The great Ibn al-Haytham, Ibn 'Abdu'llah, the great *adib* of Fez and Yaqut, the author of *Mu'jam al-Buldan* were great scribes of the time. Because of his achievement in calligraphy al-Juvaini was called *Fakhru'l-Kuttab* and Shah Jahan the Mughal emperor of India, the prophet of calligraphy.

Such being the case there was hard competition among the scribes and calligraphists; some like Yahya Ibn Adi excelled in speed writing one hundred pages in twenty four hours, others in enhancing the quality of their writing achieved name and fame.

Qutbah, who worked for Umayyad Caliphs, developed four types of writing for official correspondence namely *Jali, Tumar, Thuluthayn* and *Thulth* e.g. mighty on full scrolls, boldface (scroll type), two-thirds type and one-third type. Caliph Al-Walid preferred large-scale writing for full scrolls while 'Umar ibn 'Abd al-'Aziz in order to economizing the use of papyrus ordered for minute writing. Sa'd was the earliest monumental calligrapher of Caliph Walid's time. He wrote Quranic inscriptions in gold on the *qiblah* wall of Prophet's Mosque at Madinah and copied the *Qur'an* and some verses and episodes in a beautiful hand.

Of the early Abbasid period Ahmad ibn Abi Khalid known as *al-Ahwal al-Muharrir* (the squint-eyed clean copyist) was the greatest calligraphist of the time. He flourished under Ma'mun al-Rashid. While the beauty of the calligraphy was appreciated by the elite, scholars like Ibn Qutaybah (213-76/282-89) complained that for the sake of their beautiful hand and artistic skill the calligraphists sacrificed their scholarly objectives. *'Iraqi, Rayasi* and many other types of script were introduced under the Abbasids but very few of them have survived.

'Ali b. 'Ubayd al-Raihani (d. 322/934) was a well-known calligraphist of the Abbasid period. He introduced a type of *Naskhi* writing similar to *Muhaqqaq* which came to be known as *Raihani* after his name.

Wazir ibn Muhammad ibn 'Ali ibn Muqla (272-328/886-940) wrote a poem on calligraphy. He formulated rules for *Naskhi* character of writing and introduced or developed four forms of Arabic writing *Thulth, Muhaqqaq, Riqa'* and *Tawqi'*. He did not invent *Naskhi* as reported by Ibn Kallikan and followed by others. In calligraphy he was the disciple of al-Ahwal al-Muharrir.

Abu'l Hasan 'Ali ibn Hilal surnamed Ibn al-Bawwab (d. 413/1022 A.C.) was one of the greatest calligraphists of his age. On his death Ibn Kallikan composed the following verses:-

> "Thy loss was felt by the writers of former times, and each successive day justifies their grief.
> The ink-bottles are, therefore, black with sorrow, and the pens are rent through affliction"[7]

A great calligraphist Najam al-Din Abu Bakr Muhammad was born at Ravand near Kashan in the 12th century. He achieved mastery over seventy different styles of writing the chief among which were *Naskhi, Thulth, Riqa'* and *Muhaqqaq.* He learnt the art of calligraphy for ten years from his uncle Taj al-Din Ahmad, a great calligraphist of his time. Najm al-Din earned his livelihood by copying, illuminating and binding the copies of the *Qur'an.* He wrote a book on the principles of calligraphy and included a chapter on it in his History of the *Saljuqs.* Mahmud ibn Muhammad another maternal uncle of Najm-al-Ravandi taught calligraphy to the Saljuq King Tughril in 579/1183 and helped him in the illumination of the 30 parts of the *Qur'an* copied by Tughril himself in beautiful hand. In 585/1189 Mahmud was sent on an embassy to the Atabek Qizil Arslan of Mazandran with a quatrain written and ornamented with gilt letters by Sultan Tughril.

Ghulam Muhammad, Haft Qalami (the master of seven styles) of the Mughal court, was fond of visiting calligraphists and discussing problems of penmanship with them. Haft Qalami visited Hafiz Nurullah who had transcribed by then *Haft-band Kashi* at the request of Asaf al-Daulah **Bahadur** and was very much delighted on seeing the bold and fine varieties of the Aqa's penmanship.[8]

Mir Khalilullah Shah was greatly honoured for his penmanship. He copied the *Nau-Ras* and presented it to Ibrahim 'Adil Shah, the King of the Deccan, who gave him a seat by his side on the throne and his nobles escorted him to his residence.[9] For his calligraphy he was once offered Rupees seven hundred which he did not accept but parted with it on receiving an Arabian horse.[10]

Jamaluddin Abu Durr Yaqut b. Yaqut ibn 'Abd Allah al-Rumi al-Musta'sami (d. 698/1298 A.C.) flourished at the court of Musta'sam bi'llah the last Abbasid Caliph of Baghdad. Though the *Naskh* character was developed by Ibn Muqlah it achieved great perfection at the hand of Yaqut the greatest of *Naskh* writers.[11] His father and grandfather had also excelled in the art of calligraphy before him. According to Haji Khalifah he was never excelled by anyone. Because of his reputation the specimen copy of his calligraphy was in great demand. His copies of the *Dictionary of al-Jawhari* were sold at one hundred dinars (£50.00) each. A copy of Ibn Sina's *Shafa* he sent to Muhammad b. Tughlaq (d. 1324 A.C.), the Sultan of India, who sent two hundred million mithqals of gold coins in return which the proud calligraphist refused to accept considering it a meagre amount. A copy of the *Qur'an* transcribed by him in 688H/1289 A.C. is one of the principal treasures of Bankipur (Patna, India) Khuda Bakhsh Library.

Khwajah Mir 'Ali Tabrizi, who traced his descent from Hadrat Husain bin 'Ali was a contemporary of Amir Timur (d. 807/1405 A.C.). Although *Nasta'liq* character of writing was introduced before Mir 'Ali, still there was roughness in the style which he removed and brought perfection to the style by making it methodical in 823H/1420 A.C. He was in the service of Timur who designated him *Qiblat al-Kuttab,* model of calligraphers. He was himself very much conscious of his talents to which he referred in his poems (*Majmu'h*)[12], a copy of the collection of his selected poems, bearing Shah Jahan's autograph is preserved in the Khuda Bakhsh Library. The Mughal emperor Jahangir was a great admirer of his calligraphy for the culture of which he established a school to be followed by Mir'Imahd and othes.

The style which he initiated was developed by great calligraphists of the time like his son 'Abd Allah who taught lessons in the art of calligraphy to Maulana Ja'far of Tabriz and Maulana Azhar Tabrizi (d. 880/1475-6). The last one was entitled *ustad i-ustadan* 'master of masters. A MS. of the *Shah Namah*, copied by Azhar, was preserved in the library of Riza Shah Pahlavi of Iran. Maulana Azhar transmitted his style to his son Muhammad and his pupil Sultan 'Ali ibn Muhammad al-Mashhadi (d. 1515 A.C.)

Sultan 'Ali Mashhadi received patronage from the Timurid King Sultan Husain Mirza of Harat (1470H/1506), the patron of the great painter Bihzad. He is credited with having perfected *Nasta'liq* calligraphy. Some Timurid Kings like Baysunghur (1397-1433) and Ibrahim Sultan were themselves masters of fine penmanship. Baysunghur established an academy at Harat where worked forty painters, penmen, gilders, illuminators and bookbinders. Sultan Husain Bayqara, the last of the Timurid Kings of Harat, was another great bibliophile in whose atelier Sultan 'Ali copied manuscripts and Bihzad and his pupils adorned them with elegant miniature paintings. The tradition built up by the Timurids was followed by the Safavids in Persia and the Mughals in India.

Muhammad Husain of Tabriz was the court calligraphist of Shah Tahmasp. One of his superb MSS was in the personal collection of Rai Bahadur Jalan of Patna (India).

Mir 'Imad al-Husaini of Qazvin wrote in a *Nasta'liq* hand of great excellence. It achieved unapproachable mastery of the *Nasta'liq* style for which he was lavished with honour and money although he cared little for them because of his pride in his talent. The Safavid ruler Shah 'Abbas I of Persia (1587-1625) keenly desired to own a copy of the *Shahnamah* transcribed by him. The Shah sent him seventy *tumans* with a request to copy the epic for him. After one year the Shah sent for the copy. Mir 'Imad gave seventy lines in return for the gift he had received. The Shah felt offended and returned the seventy lines demanding seventy *tumans* back. Each line the calligraphist sold to his disciples for one *tuman* each and returned the amount to Shah 'Abbas I. This impertinence enraged the Shah all the more and the artist was murdered by the King's slave Mansur Misgar in 1024H/1615 A.C. The calligraphist received the highest approbration from Kings of distant realms. Jahangir, the Mughal emperor of India, wept for him on receiving the news of his murder and was prepared to pay his weight in pearls to Shah 'Abbas had he been sent to the Mughal emperor. Shah Jahan was so fond of collecting the specimen copies of his calligraphy that whoever presented him with a genuine work of 'Imad he was conferred with the rank of *Yaksadi* (Centurion,

Commander of one hundred horse).[13] A copy of the *Tuhfatu'l-abrar* of Jami transcribed by Mir 'Imad is in Istanbul. He belonged to the group of five great calligraphists of Iran, the other four being Sultan 'Ali, Mir 'Ali, Shah Mahmud and Muhammad Husain of Tabriz. He was a Saiyid of Qazvin and studied with his master 'Isa, a painter of Qazvin, Malik Daylami and Mulla Muhammad Husain of Tabriz. Some specimens of Mir 'Imad's writings are preserved in the Khuda Bakhsh Library, Patna.

Mulla Muhammad Amin of Kashan was a great master of *Nasta'liq* writing. He was employed as superintendent of the Mughul noble Khan Khanan'Abd al-Rahim's library on a monthly salary of Rs. 4,000/-.[14] Scribes and artists of Khan Khanan received also *jagirs* (fiefs).

Among the best of the great penmen of the Mughal court was 'Abd al-Rashid Daylami better known as Aqa Rashid. He was the son of Mir 'Imad's sister and his own student. Improving upon Mir'Ali's style he gained wide reputation in Persia for his art. After the murder of his maternal uncle he travelled to India in Shah Jahan's time. He was appointed as a writing-master in *Nasta'liq* to his son Prince Dara Shikuh. Most of his life he lived at Akbarabad and was buried there in 1081H/1670 A.C. His calligraphy was valuable and graceful. A specimen of his beautiful *Nasta'liq* is preserved in Khuda Bakhsh Library of Bankipur (Patna). Among the followers of Mir 'Ali's *Khatt* (writing), Mahmud b. Ishaq Shahabi achieved great name. Of his writings *Diwan i-Shahzadah Kamran* is in the Khuda Bakhsh Library.

The name and fame of calligraphists meant money to forgers. The names of renowned calligraphists were exploited by later artists especially by their students assigning their own writings in their names. Amir Razwi imitated his master Aqa 'Abd al-Rashid's style and assigned his own writings in his name. Aqa's death anniversary was observed in every Muharram at Akbarabad which was attended by artists from Delhi and other towns. On the 4th of Muharram a lively gathering used to take place at the house of Shah Waris 'Ali (d. 1227H/1812 A.C.). He was a good calligraphist and an admirer of Aqa Rashid. Maulana Khwajah Muhammad also assigned his writings in the name of his master Mulla Mir 'Ali of which fact the latter was aware.[15]

22

Saiyid 'Ali Khan (*Jawahir Raqam*) bin Aqa Muqim came to India from Tabriz. The Mughal emperor Aurangzib employed him to teach calligraphy to the princes of the Royal family. He wrote after the style of Mir 'Imad and Aqa Rashid very elegantly. For some time he worked as a curator of the Mughal Imperial Library and died suffering from madness in the Deccan in 1094H/1683 A.C.

Pen, Ink and Writing Materials:- The calligraphists were very particular about their writing materials. Reed pen or *qalam* having fine cut served the purpose of broader nib to write bold stroke and its edge being smooth it glided with ease over the paper enabling the hand to give fine swing and swell to the curved lines which is one of the chief beauties of the Arabic Persian writing.

As the beauty of writing depended very much on ink, it was prepared with great care and was made shining and durable by mixing chemicals. Ink was made up of lamp-black and vinegar or well beaten up and mixed with red ochre or yellow arsenic and camphor. The ink of *'Shir Khurma'* was used in writing the copy of the famous Dictionary of Abu Nasr Isma'il b. Hammad al-Jawhari dated 648H/1250 A.C., which is preserved in the library of Aligarh Muslim University (India).

Information on writing materials before the introduction and wide circulation of paper we obtain from the traditions concerning the missionary epistles employed by the Prophet, the accounts of the collection of the *Surahs* (verses) of the *Qur'an* under the presidentship of Zaid ibn Thabit (12H/633-4 A.C.) and the *Fihrist* of Ibn Nadim.

Adim (leather) was the principal material for writing during the time of the Prophet and he used it in |writing letters to various kings calling upon them to accept Islam. *'Asib* (palm leaf) was another material used by the Prophet in sending a missionary letter to the *'Udhra*. Pieces of camel's bones *('azam)*, especially *adla'* (ribs) and *aktaf* (shoulder blades), were used as writing materials by the early Muslims. Wooden tablets (*takhtah*) and flat white stones (*lakhaf*) were also used sometimes. *Khazaf* or *shaqaf* (pot sherds or broken pieces of porcelain) were used for short notes in ancient time by the Greeks, Copts and Persians, but were rarely used by the Muslims.

The use of parchment called *raqq* and *jild* (finished leather) because of its high price was limited to the writing of documents and copying of the *Qur'an*. It was used in al-Maghrib for copying scriptures as late as the last part of the 4th and beginning of the 5th centuries of Hijra era. The great 'Arab geographer Maqdisi records of its use in writing documents and copying the *Qur'an* in North Africa.

Papyrus called *Qirtas Misri* was made of a plant of the sedge family in Egypt from where it spread all over the world. Even after the introduction of paper it continued to be used as late as the middle of the 10th century A.C. The latest papyrus documents preserved in the Khedivial and Vienna libraries are dated 319H/931 and 323/935 A.C. respectively. It was replaced by paper a cheap and suitable material for writing. The earliest Baghdad MS. written on paper is dated 256H/870 A.C. and the Cairo MS. no. 6546 is dated 265H/878-9 A.C. Great technique was used in preparing smooth and coloured paper.

To improve the quality of the calligraphy the paper was pressed and made smooth by placing it in a well-levelled board of chestnut wood and polishing it with an egg of crystal of about half a pound's weight. The Chinese were the first people in the world to practice the art of manufacturing paper from silk. After the conquest of Samarqand in 704 A.C. the Arabs came into contact with the Chinese. In 706 the art of making paper from cotton was introduced at Makkah by one Yusuf'Amr.[16] The 'Arab general Zayyad ibn Salih as ransom got the Muslims trained in the art of paper making by the Chinese taken captives in the battle of the Talas River fought in Turkistan in 96H/751 A.C. and set these prisoners free to embark on Chinese junks ready for sail in the Persian Gulf.[17] According to al-Nadim, the author of *al-Fihrist,* there existed seven different kinds of paper in the 2nd half of the first century of the Hijra era. In India good quality paper came from Kashmir. According to Idrisi, Spain supplied good quality paper to North Africa as early as the 12th century A.C. Arabic MSS. on cotton paper is still preserved in the Escorial Library of Spain and some of them are dated as early as the tenth century. Paper was manufactured from cotton, linen and *shahdanj* (*cañamo*) at San Felipe (Jativa) and Valencia. In early thirteenth century its manufacture was introduced by Alfonso X (d. 1284 A.C.) in Castile from where it passed to France in 1270 A.C. The example of France was followed by other European countries — Italy, Germany and

England.[18]

1. Ibn Khallikan, II, p.284; Hughes, Thomas Patrick, *Dictionary of Islam,* London, 1885, p.680.
2. Moritz, *Arabic Writing* in *Encyclopaedia of Islam,* Vol. I, pp.381-2.
3. *Dictionary of Islam,* pp.683-84.
4. *Indian Antiquary,* Jan. 1875, p.28.
5. Ibn Khaldun, I, pp.350-53; Vol. II, p.384.
6. Popes Arthur Upha, *A Survey of Persian Art,* Vol, II, Oxford, 1939, p.1733; cf. *Islam Calligraphy in Medieval India* by the author is JASB, Dacca, 1979-81, pp.249, 254.
7. *Dictionary of Islam,* p.692.
8. Ghulam Muhammad *Tadhkirah-i-Khushnavisan,* pp.45, 46.
9. *Ibid.* pp.79, 80.
10. *Ibid.* p.81.
11. *Les Calligraphes et les Miniaturistes,* by Huart, p.85.
12. Tadhkirah-i-Khushnavisan, pp.52-42.
13. *Ibid.* pp.92, 93.
14. *Islamic Culture*, Hider Ahad, Oct. 1931, p.627.
15. *Tadhkirah-i-Khushnavisan,* p.80.
16. Al-Ghazzal and Casirqueted by Lue viardot, *Historia de los Arabes y de los Morosde Espana,* Barcelona, 1844, p.239.
17. Needham, Joseph, *Science and Civilisation in China,* Vol. I, Cambridge 1954, p.125, Fatimi, S.Q., *Mashriq-i-Ba'id men Tulu' Islam,* Lahore, 1978, pp.38-9.
18. Already composed see above.

1

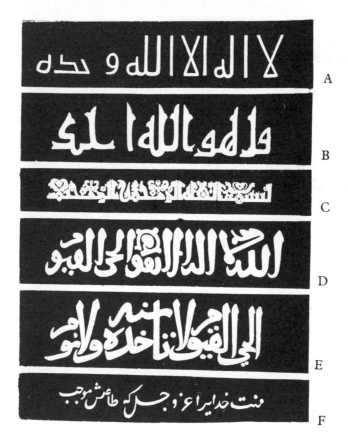

A

B

C

D

E

F

a. Simple Kufic A.C., AH (790 AD), Simple Kufic is characterised by straight vertical strokes and angular forms of letters.

b. Folitated Kufic AH 341 (952 AC). The vertical strokes end in leaves and half-palmettes.

c. Floriated Kufic AH 243 (848 AC). The ending of the letters is enhanced by the floral designs and half-palmettes, while the round forms are rendered as rosettes.

d. Naskhi AH 684 (1285 AC) Naskhi is a cursive form of Arabic writing, here the verticals are not so important; some of the foliation has has been taken over from Kufic.

e. Thuluth (1348 AC). Thuluth is a more cursive and more elegant form than Naskhi. The words are placed above each other in two or even more lines.

f. Nastaliq AH 950 (1543 AC). In Nastaliq the horizontal lines and round forms are exaggerated, dots casually placed, lines are not always straight, all of which make the Nastaliq a very elegant form of writing.

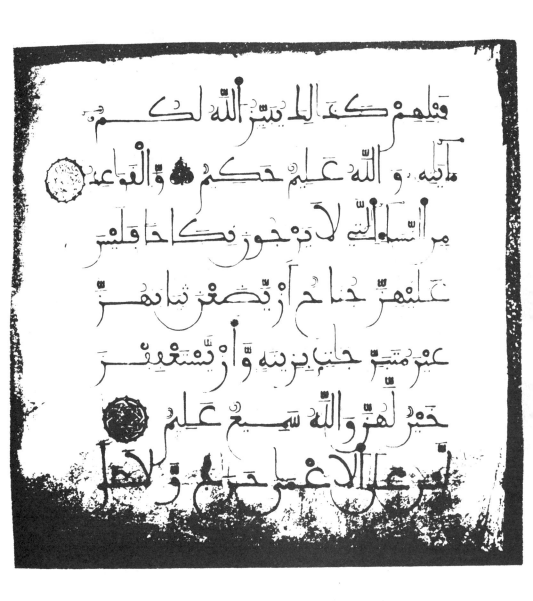

Page from 11th Century Quran North Africa.

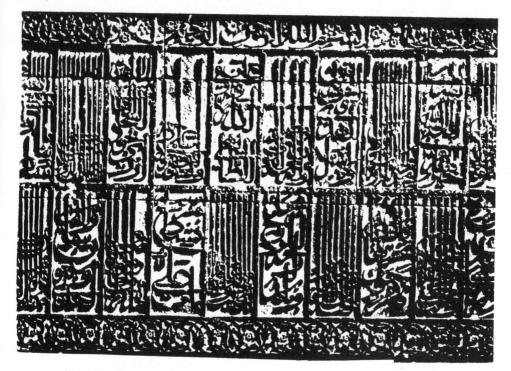

Detail of a Commemorative stone from the palace of Barbak Shah, Gaur, Bengal, mid-fifteenth century. Photograph courtesy of the University Museaum, Philadelphia.

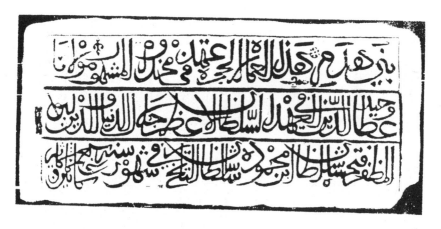

Jalalud Din Fath Shah, 887 A. H. Hetam Khan, Rajshahi.

Egypt; fourteenth century H. 24 cm W. 23.8 cm The Textile
Museum.

1 MUHAQEQ 2 SINBOLY 3 TAGRA 4 KUFFI QADEEM 5 MAGRIBI 6 IJAZA 7 JLI AL-DEWANI

8 ROQHA 9 DEWANI 10 KUFFI MOZAHIR 11 THOLTH 12 TALEEQ 13 KUFFI MADFOOR

14 NASKH 15 KUFFI MORABBA

SECTION II

'ARAB LIBRARIES

CHAPTER I

UMAYYAD AND ABBASID LIBRARY

The beginning of Muslim libraries like those of the Jews and the Christians goes back to the collection of religious books. As synagogue, church and monastic libraries changed into public school, college, university libraries of today, the Mosque library of the early Muslim period developed into the Madrasah and University libraries of the middle ages. By the time Prophet Muhammad (peace of God be upon him) died there were only a few verses (*Surahs*) of the Holy *Qur'an* in written form, some copies of letters sent to various rulers calling upon them to accept Islam and also copies of some treaties concluded with people of Madinah and other places to be preserved in Muslim libraries.

During the time of the early caliphs, the Holy *Qur'an* was compiled under the Chairmanship of Zayd ibn Thabit in 30H/651 A.C. to be enlisted as the first book in the history of Muslim libraries to which were added copies of some treaties made with the people conquered during the *Khilafat* period after the demise of the Prophet Muhammad. More than this could not be done as the Muslims were pre-occupied in the expansion of Islam and in setting up their administrative affairs.

Umayyad Library:- Although the collection of books and papers on history, biography, laws and traditions was begun as early as the days of Prophet and righteous Caliphs still the building up of libraries and translation of books from Greek into Arabic began under the Umayyads. By the time the Banu Umayyah came to power the situation had improved and the Muslims came into close contact with the Egyptians, Syrians, Greeks and Persians, but they were yet so busy with internal and external affairs, viz economic and social problems that they hardly found time to devote to the establishment of literary institutions except to the introduction and writing of a number of books on grammar, religious traditions, historical and geographical accounts, postal guides and translation of some Greek works into Arabic.

With the expansion of Islam when the non-Arabs accepted Islam and committed some orthographical mistakes in reciting their Holy scripture, Basrah and Kufah schools had to introduce rules of grammar for the new converts from the time of the third Caliph Hadrat 'Uthman. The first historical work *Kitab al-Muluk-wa-Akhbar al- Mada'in* was written by 'Adb bin Shari'ah b. *Mu'awiyah.* The latter's grandson Khalid b. Yazid learnt chemistry from the Greek scholar of Alexandria namely Marionis and Istafan al-Qadim translated for him some Greek works into Arabic. Khalid also had a number of books on philosophy and astronomy translated into Arabic from Greek and Hebrew to enrich his own collection.[1] He himself wrote books like *Kitab al-Harat, Kitab al-Sahifah al-Kabir* and *Kitab al-Sahifah al-Saghir.*[2]

The *Tafsir* (commentary) of the *Qur'an* written by S'id b. Jubair was preserved in the royal library of 'Abd al-Malik b. Marwan, who had engaged scholars for writing books on various subjects. Under 'Umar b. 'Abd al-'Aziz the collection of traditions was made by Abu Bakr b. Hazm Ansari, the teacher of Imam Zuhri, and 'Asim b. 'Umar b. Qatadah. Ansari gave lessons on *Maghazi* and *Manaqib.* A book of his royal library written by Hakim Masir Joyah was translated from the Syriac. On the death of Walid b. Yazid when his collections were transferred from the library, the books written by Imam Zuhri alone had to be transported laden on the backs of several asses and camels.[3] Under the Umayyads besides Khalid b Yazith others were interested in building up their private libraries. Abu 'Amr ibn al-'Ala al-Ma'arri (d. 156/770), who had flourished towards the close of the Umayyad rule, is recorded by Ibn Khallikan to have collected books filling one of his rooms up to the ceiling.[4]

Abbasid Library:- The Umayyad collections were appropriated by the Abbasids after their overthrow and the private collections became richer and richer. The Abbasids patronised art and learning, opened translation bureau and established *madrasahs* and libraries. Throughout the four years of his rule the Abbasid Caliph al-Saffah remained occupied in state affairs finding little time to devote to literary activities. His brother and successor Abu Ja'far al-Mansur (754-75 A.C.), however, having established his dynasty firmly devoted his times to literary pursuits. He opened a translation bureau, collected Greek, Persian and Sanskrit works in hundreds on philosophy, medicine, astronomy and other sciences and had them translated into Arabic. An Indian work on astronomy namely *Siddhanta* was received at Baghdah in 771 A.C., and translated into Arabic by Muhammad ibn al-Fazari. This was later used by al-Khwarizmi in the preparation of his astronomical tables, called *Zijj*. Besides the translation work, the composition of original books was also taken up seriously under the patronage of the Abbasid Caliphs.

As a result of the royal patronage to learning, public interest in the sale and purchase of books and papers increased and bookshops were opened in a number of cities. A special market called *Suq al-Warraqin* grew up in Baghdad. It had about one hundred such shops. In the absence of printing presses, calligraphists and copyists were employed in libraries and shops to copy rare and valuable works to meet the increasing demand of scholars for such books and to copy text books for students and other customers thus standardising the prices of books and creating interest in the readers on large scale for building up their personal collections, some being scholars and teachers needed them, others being philanthropists decorated with them their drawing rooms. Among the libraries which grew up thus were of three types, mosque libraries, royal libraries and private collections.

Bayt al-Hikmah:- In 145H/762 A.C. the foundation of the round city of Baghdad was laid by the Abbasid Caliph Abu Ja'far Mansur (d. 775 A.C.). This was the town which developed as a centre of Islamic civilization within the first fifty years of the Abbasid rule and reached its zenith under Harun and Ma'mun. The Abbasid *Bayt al-Hikmah* was a parallel institution to the Academy of *Han-Lin-Yuan* of Ming Huang, the Chinese emperor of T'ang Dynasty. The Chinese academy functioned up to the end of the Ming Dynasty (15th century)[6] The first institution of higher scientific studies among the Arabs was *Bayt al-Hikmah* a combination of library, academy and translation bureau. It was founded on the bank of the Tigris at Baghdad by Harun al-Rashid in 830 A.C. The translation work under royal patronage had started earlier under Mansur. In the translation bureau works were translated into Arabic from Greek. Sanskrit and other non-Arabic languages and they have been enlisted by Haji Khalifah in his *Kashf al-Zunun* and by Ibn Nadim in *al-Fihrist*. In

34

the conquest of Anqirah and 'Umuriah a rich collection of books was obtained which Harun entrusted to his Christian physician Yuhanna b. Aswiah to translate into Arabic. The famous geographer Yaqut states that 'Allan transcribed books in this institution for the Barmaki officials and Abbsdid Caliph Harun and later also for his son Ma'mun al-Rashid.

The Abbasid Caliph Ma'mun engaged Ya'qub b. Ishaq 'al-Kindi, who wrote 282 books and memoirs on medicine, philosophy, music etc., for translating Aristotle's works into Arabic. Translators were generally paid in the weight of their translation and each copy of their works was sealed and signed by Ma'mun himself. Rare books were collected from distant places of Egypt, Syria, Persia and India. Hajjaj b. al-Batriq and the principal of the college, Salam by name, were sent to the Byzantine countries by Ma'mun to collect books of their choice. Qusta b. Luqa on his own went to the Greek countries in search of books. Hunain b. Ishaq went in search of *Kitab al-Burhan* to Palestine, Egypt and Syria and obtained only half of it at Damascus. Ibn Abi al-Harish, a famous book binder of the time, was engaged in the *Baytu'l Hikmah*. Hindu, Parsi, Christian and Jews besides the Muslims were on the staff of *Baytu'l Hikmah*. Duban, the Indian physician, Hunain ibn Ishaq, Yuhanna b. Aswiah, Qusta b. Luqa, Sahl b. Harun and Abu Ja'far Yahya b. Adi all worked in the *Baytu'l Hikmah*. Most of the employees received Rs. 2,500/- (F125,00) at the present rate.[7] The famous scientist mathematician Muhammad b. Musa al-Khwarizmi, who invented algebra and wrote the *Kitab al-Jabr Wa'l Muqabilah* on the request of Ma'mun, was also attached to this institution.[8]

Among the old rare collection of *Bayt al-Hikmah* was a letter of Prophet's grandfather 'Abd al-Muttalib written on leather,[8] the *Almagest* of Batlimus which was translated into Arabic and a rare work consisting of about 100 pages written by Naushirawsan'-*wazir*.[9] This institution survived under different names up to the 12th century but it was overshadowed by the Nizamiyah college founded by Nizam al-Mulk Tusi in the 11th century A.C.

Later when political power passed from the hands of the Abbasid Caliphs to those of the army generals and *sultans*, the Saljuqs and the Buwayhids topped the list in patronising learning and science.

35

Nizamiyah:- Nizam al-Mulk Tusi, the prime minister of the Saljuq Sultan Malikshah, established a chain of *madrasahs* at Baghdad, Basrah, Mosul, Isfahan, and other towns. The most famous of these colleges was that of Baghdad. The Nizamiyah of Baghdad was founded in 457H/1065 A.C. and opened in Dhiqa'd 459/ Sept. 1067. It cost Tusi 60,000 dinars. The first professor of this college was Abu Nasr ibn al-Sabbagh who was dismissed after twenty days and Abu Ishaq al-Shirazi was appointed as its principal in his place. The professor who was called *Shaykh* had under him two or more *mu'ids* (repeaters) to read over the lecture after class and explain it to the less gifted students.[10] It was in this college that the famous mystic al-Ghazzali lectured for four years (1091-5 A.C.)[11] and because of his learning and scholarship he became chief *mudarris* at an early age of thirty four only. Scholars like al-Mawardi and Ibn Mubarak were associated with it in 1104 and 1184 A.C. respectively and it was here that among the later teachers the biographer of Salahuddin Ayyubi, namely Baha'uddin delivered lectures. Shaykh Sa'di was one of the renowned students of this college. It was a theological *madrasah* particularly for the study of Ash'ari and Shafi'i rites. 'Ali ibn Muhammad, a teacher of this institution, who taught grammar, was accused of following Shi'ism and dismissed.[12] It was visited by travellers like Ibn Jubayr in 1185 and Ibn Battutah in 1327 A.C. According to Ibn Jubayr there were thirty colleges in Baghdad, all supported by endowments and Nizamiya was the most important of all. Teachers and writers received fixed salary and the students were granted stipends all from the endowed properties. The annual expenditure of the college amounted to sixty to seventy million dinars.

The library attached to the Nizamiyah college had magnificent collections, which were mostly bequeathed *waqfs* and gifts. Muhib al-Din ibn al-Najjar at Baghdad, according to the historian Ibn al-Athir, endowed two of his personal collections valuing one thousand dinars to its library. Whenever Nazamu'l Mulk Tusi came to Baghdad he used to visit this library and devoted sometimes to the reading of books. He was the man who wrote *Siyasat Namah* or *Siyar al-Mulk*, which was prescribed for long for civil service examination at London. He was murdered by a madman in 485H/1092 A.C.

Abu Zakariya Tabrizi was appointed as a librarian of Nizamiyah **Madrasah** on a very high salary. He was followed by Ya'qub b.

Sulaiman Asqara'i as librarian. In 1116 A.C. the institution caught fire but the books were removed undamaged. A new building for the library was constructed at the order of Caliph al-Nasir (1180-1225), who donated to it his own collections of thousands of books. It was a very rich library having valuable and magnificent collections although the number of books is not known. It survived the catastrophe which befell the city of Baghdad during Hulagu Khan's capture of the Abbasid capital in 1258 A.C. and later invasions of the Tartars to be finally merged with her sister institution Mustansiriyah in 1393, two years after the capture of Baghdad by Timur.

Mustansiriyah:- The college under the name of Mustansiriyah was founded on the eastern side of Baghdad by the Abbasid Caliph, last but one, al-Mustansir Bi'llah (1226-1242 A.C.) in 625H/1228 A.C. and completed in six years. Rare and valuable books laden on 160 camels were transferred to it from the Imperial Library. Its ruins on the banks of the Tigris are still visible. It topped the list of many *madrashahs* founded by Mustansir. A hospital and a library were attached to it. Ibn Battutah gives a detailed description of its building and describes the function of the seminary and library.[13] On its pattern the early European universities were developed.[14]

The library possessed rare and valuable works on various subjects. There was a good arrangement of open shelf system. Students had free access to the well arranged shelves and were allowed to use even the rare manuscripts. Beside stack rooms and reading rooms there were also lecture rooms for teaching astronomy and other sciences in addition to traditions of the Prophet. The library was visited daily by Mustansir Caliph.

On the very first day of the opening ceremony of the college Caliph Mustansir Bi'llah donated his own personal collection and appointed men to do accession and classification work. The Caliph continued donating books from time to time. Donation of books was also received from scholars and philanthropists. At one time it contained about 40,000 volumes. It has been described as a unique collection by historians like Ibn al-Athir. The library work was supervised by trustworthy persons including his son Prince al-Musta'sim, who, on his accession to the *Khilafat*, took the same keen interest in the affairs of the library and the college as his father had been doing.

The library was visited by distinguished scholars and travellers. It operated until the Mongols entered Baghdad and destoryed it. A large number of its collections were removed by Hulagu Khan to Maraghah where famous astronomer Nasir al-Din al-Tusi had laid the foundation of an observatory in 648H/1250 A.C. A manuscript of Mustansiriyah library is now to be found in the Bibliotheca Nationale, Paris.

Libraries under the Buwayhids (945-1055 A.C.):- Like the Saljuqs. the Buwayhids also patronised art and literature. Bakhtiyar and Habashi, the two sons of the Buwayhid Amir Mu'izz al-Dawlah, were lovers of learning and vied with each other for the acquisition of documents. Among the confiscated property of the defeated Habashi was his library at Basrah containing 15,000 books exclusive of unbound volumes and loose sheets.[15]

The greatest of the Buwayhid sultans, 'Adud al-Dawlah (972-82) was a great bibliophile. He had his library at his capital city of Shiraz housed in a separate building and administered by a *Wakil* (trustee), *Khazin* (treasurer) and *Mushrif* (collector), all chosen from the trustworthy people of Shiraz. It was visited by Maqdisi, the famous georgrapher, during the time of 'Adud al-Dawlah. he left behind its vivid description. The geographer says that the books were well arranged on shelves with separate cupboards and catalogues of books subjectwise and adds that the library contained the copies of all the books published up to his time.[16] The minute details of the Sultan's library are given by another famous geographer Yaqut in the following words:

> "The library consists of one long vaulted room, annexed to which are store rooms. The prince had made along the large room and the store chambers, scaffoldings about the height of a man three yards wide, of decorated wood which have shelves from top to bottom. The books are arranged on the shelves and for every branch of learning there are separate scaffolds. There are also catalogues in which all the titles of the books are entered. I also saw the ventilation chamber to which the water was carried by pipes, surrounding it on every side in circulation."[17]

Commenting on Yaqut's observation Olga Pinto remarks that such arrangement of ventilation led to the books being infested by vermin. The shelf guides in the great library of Shiraz appear to have been more informative than their modern counterparts in as much as they also indicated the incomplete or mutilated works on the shelves, a duty proposed by the library catalogue today.[18] The library of the Buwayhids was intact until the time of al-Hariri (d. 122 A.C.), who mentioned it in his *Maqamat*.

Abud al-Dawlah (d. 367-72H/Aug 977-June 980) sultan of Shiraz founded a magnificent library named *Khazinatset Kutub*. Besides a considerable number of books it possessed, the library was noted for its fine buildings, furniture and arrangements. The building was surrounded by parks and roofed with domes. There were 350 rooms and partitioning. The books were arranged on the shelves with a complete catalogue.

Sharaf al-Dawlah, son of Adadud al-Dawlah, an astronomer built up a new library of his own at Shiraz. The Buwayhid libraries at Basrah and Ramhurmuz were also visited by Maqdisi. Readers at both the libraries were given stipends. The collection of Basrah was bigger and richer than that of Ramhurmuz and the latter was the seat of the Mu'tazilite learning. The last Buwayhid Sultan Majd al-Dawlah had his library at Rayy which was occupied by Sultan Mahmud of Ghaznah in July 1029, its collection on Mu'tazilite philosophy was burnt, and other books, fifty loads in number, were removed.

The Buwayhid wazirs also had rich collections of books. Ustad Abu'l Fadl ibn al-'Amid, the wazir of Rukn al-Dawlah, had one hundred camel loads of books under the charge of the famous historian Abu 'Ali Miskawayh. The rich collection of Sahib Isma'il ibn 'Abbad, the wazir of Mu'ayyid al-Dawlah and Fakhr al-Dawlah, had 400 camel loads of books which were catalogued in ten big volumes at Rayy, but were destroyed by Sultan Mahmud's soldiers in July 1029 A.C.[19] Among the other important libraries opened to the public although private were *Daru'l'Ilm* at Mosul founded by Abu'l Qasim Ja'far ibn Muhammad ibn Hamdan al-Mosuli (854-934 A.C.), a library attached to the *madrasah* at the tomb of Imam Abu Hanifah, three miles north of Baghdad, and the library of Zaydi's Mosque, the one was founded by Muhammad ibn Mansur al 'Amid al-Khwarizmi in 1066 A.C. and the other one by al-Sharif al-'Zaydi (d. 1179). The Abbasid Caliph al-Nasir li-Din Allah (1180-1225 A.C.) built a library attached to the tomb of his Queen Saljuqah Khatun at Basrah Gate in Baghdad.[20] The libraries of Basrah, Mosul and Mashhad Abu Hanifah contained magnificent collections and were opened to the public. Yaqut collected materials for three years for his dictionary *Mu'jam al-Buldan* from the libraries of Marv and Khwarizm until 1220 he had to flee at the approach of the Mongol hordes under Chingiz Khan, who destroyed the city and burnt these libraries.[21]

Besides the royal libraries at Baghdad and public Buwayhid Sultan's libraries at Shiraz and elsewhere, there were thousands of private collections in the Abbasid empire, of the caliphs and their wazirs like those of Yahya al-Barmaki (d. 805 A.C.), Ibn al-Zayyat (d. 847 A.C.), al-Fath ibn Khaqan (d. 861 A.C.), al-Qasim ibn 'Ubayd Allah (d. 903), al-Khunduri (d. 1063 A.C.), Ibn Hubahrah (d. 1149 A.C.) and Ibn al-'Alqami (d. 1258 A.C.). Their biographical details given by contemporary and later historians and geographers became testimony to the fact that these personal collections possessed many rare manuscripts and were well-staffed including scribes and calligraphists to copy rare and valuable works and artists to illuminate and illustrate them with drawings and miniatures. Among the scholars, who had rich collections, that of the blind poet and philosopher Abu 'Amr ibn al-'Ala Ma'arri (d. 770 A.C.) was very rich but this he himself destroyed when he set himself aside from worldly pleasures. Sufyan al-Thawri, Waqidi and Isam'il had their private libraries. 'Amr ibn Bahr al-Jahiz (d. 868 A.C.), a great literary personality of his days, was in the habit of going through all books cover to cover in his collection and visited regularly shops for more and more rare works.

FOOTNOTES

1. cf. Abdus Subbuh Qasmi, *Libraries in the Early Islamic World*, Peshawar, 1958, pp. 2-3
2. Muhammad Zubair, *Islami Kutub Khane*, Delhi 1961, p. 33
3. *Rasa'il Shibli*, p.29; *Islami Kutub Khane*, pp. 33-4.
4. Abdus Subbuh, p. 3
5. Needham, Joseph — *Science and Civilization in China, Vol: I, Cambridge 1954, pp. 125, 127, 135.*
6. Shibli, Al-Ma'mun, Azamgarh, 1963, p. 168; Ya'quli, II, 486.
7. cf. *Rasalah Burhan*, Delhi, Vol. 45, p. 173; Nicholson, p. 359; Hitti, P. K. — *History of the Arabs*, pp. 310, 410.
8. cf. *Rasa'il Shibli*, p. 32
9. Muhammad Zubair, *Islami Kutub Khane*, Delhi, 1961, p. 74.

10. Ibn Khallikan, III, II, p.130.
11. *Ibid.* I, pp. 43-9, II, p.276.
12. *Ibid.* III, pp. 435-7
13. *Ibid,* Vol. II, pp. 108-9.
14. Levy, Reuben, *A Baghdad Chronicle,* 1929, p. 193.
15. Miskawayh, *Tajarib,* II, 331
16. Maqdisi, 449
17. Yaqut, V. p. 446.
18. *The Libraries of the Arabs during the time of Abbasids, Islamic Culture,* Vol. III, 1929, pp. 227-229.
19. Yaqut, II, p.315; cf. Mafizullah Kabir, *Libraries and Academies during the Baghdad Period* (946-1055) in *Islamic Culture,* Vol. XXXIII, pp. 31-33.
20. cf. A. S. Qasimi, p. 7
21. Hitti, *History of the Arabs,* pp. 413-4

22, 23, 24 **to follow**

CHAPTER II

FATIMID LIBRARY

Egypt with its proud city and port Alexandria was conquered by the 'Arab Muslims in 642 A.D. Alexandria capitulated on favourable terms and remained the North African centre of Hellenic studies in philosophy, medicine and mathematics. It was only during the time of the Umayyad Caliph 'Umar b. 'Abd al-'Aziz (718-20) that its university moved to Antioch from where its influence spread to 'Iraq and Persia and Muslim culture developed at Cairo *(al Qahirah)*, the newly built city of the Fatimids.[1]

When the 'Abbasid power was decaying in the East and Umayyad authority was re-established in Spain, the Fatimids rose to power in North Africa. Their general Jawhar conquered Egypt for the Fatimid Caliph Mu'izz and founded Cairo. The Muslim culture and civilization reached its Zenith during the time of al-'Aziz (975-96), son of Mu'izz who founded a big library called *Khaza'in al-Qusur* consisting of forty rooms. There were 1600,000 books and booklets of which 600,000 were books and dealt with theology, grammar, dictionary, tradition, history, geography, astronomy, chemistry. Of these 6,000 books were on mathematics and astronomy alone. There were thirty copies of the *Kitab al-'Ayn* of Khalil b. Ahmad including a copy in original, twelve copies of the *Ta'rikh Tabari* and 2,000 copies of the *Qur'an* copied by famous calligraphists. There were two *Kurrahs* of the earth (globes) one made of silver at a cost of 3,000 dinars and another of brass made by Batlimus. The Library was open for the teachers, scholars and students of Cairo. Its collection was transferred to the Public Library of Daru'l 'Ilm founded by Hakim in 395/1004. Jami' Azhar was founded by the caliph Mu'izz (1358-65/968-75). During the time of 'Aziz the al-Azhar Mosque Library contained 200,000 books.[2]

Al-Ḥākim son of 'Azīz established his library at Cairo in 395/1004 attached to the Hall of learning (*Daru'l 'Ilm* or *Daru'l Ḥikmah*) which imparted free education and supported teachers, scholars and students with endowments. It contained 600,000 volumes or at least 100,000 the minimum out of which 2,400 were the illuminated copies of the *Qur'an* and 18,000 books on ancient learning. The rest of the collections dealt with jurisprudence, grammar, rhetoric, history, biography, astronomy and chemistry. There were several copies of some books. Thus there were more than twenty copies of the *Ta'rikh Tabari* including one copy written by Tabari himself, more than thirty copies of Khalil's *Kitāb al-'Ayn* including one copy in the original and 100 copies of *Kitāb al-Jamhirah bi ibn Daridah.*[3] They were kept on the shelves of almirahs under lock and key. At the entrance of each row a list of books was hung.[4] Besides these there were a large number of books in the library of *al-Azhar Madrasah*.

The Fatimid royal library was specially enriched during the time of al-Hākim, son of 'Azīz, who established *Dār al-'Ilm* or *Dār al-Hikmah* (House of Wisdom or Science) near Western Palace *(Bāb al-Tabābin)* on the 8th Jumada II 395/25th March 1004 and shifted the library to this institution which was a combination of library, academy and auditorium. Agents were sent abroad to collect rare books for this institution. According to Maqrīzī, a renowned historian of Egypt, it contained 1,600,000 volumes dealing with various subjects, *Qur'an*, astronomy, grammer, lexicography, medicine, science, literature and exquisite calligraphy. According to Asāmah b. Murthid, Qādī Abū Yūsuf was allowed by Hākim to take away many rare books according to his choice from al-Hākim's library.[5] Administrative staff and teachers were appointed, students were given endowments and supplied with books and inks. Even members of the public were allowed to use the library. The moderate annual budget amounted to 275 dinars. Some details given by Maqrīzī are furnished below:

Librarians' salary	48 dinars
Other Servants' salary	15 dinars
Paper for the copyists	90 dinars
Paper, ink and pens	12 dinars
Abbadani matting	10 dinars
Water	12 dinars
Repair of the curtains	1 dinar
Repair of torn and damaged books	12 dinars
Felt curtains for winter use	5 dinars
Carpets for winter use	4 dinars[4]

Due to political instability the rich collection of the Fatimid library suffered a great disaster and in 1068 A.C. 25 camel loads of books of this library were sold for only 100,000 dinars by Wazīr Abu'l Faraj to pay his soldiery. A few months after this incident the rest of it was plundered and destroyed by the Turkish soldiers when the Caliph Mustansir was defeated and the soldiers entered the palace. Many books were thrown into the Nile or burnt to ashes. Fine leather bindings of other books were torn and used in making shoes. The torn Manuscripts were collected in a place which became known as *Talal al-Kutub* (Hill of the books) and covered by sand in the course of time. Books were again collected by the later Fatimid rulers and by the time Ṣalāḥ al-Dīn Ayyūbī entered Cairo Victorious in 567/1171 there were a few lakhs of volumes in the Fatimid Imperial Library of which he gave 120,000 copies to his learned Minister Qāḍī al-Fadil who preserved them in his library attached to Madrasah Fāḍiliah.[7]

There were also private collections among which mention may be made of two Jewish libraries and those of an 'Arab Prince and an Egyptian physician. In the 11th century the Fatimid Prince, Maḥmūd al-Dawlah ibn Fatik, a great collector and scribe, built up a good library and passed most of his time in reading and writing without attending much to his family, who, on his death, threw many of his books in anger into a large water basin damaging a considerable number of them. The library attached to Fāḍiliyah Madrasah was rich and was among those highly spoken of by historians and geographers like Ibn al-Athīr and Maqdisī etc. The collection of the poet-physician al-Mu'arif who wrote a commentary on Aristotle in 1139 A.C. was also very rich and contained thousands of volumes on various subjects with copious notes, the contents and the name of al-Mu'arrif. Of the personal collections one of the most important one was the Mahmūdiah Library of Cairo founded by Jamāluddin Maḥmūd b. 'Alī a courtier of Sulṭān Malik Zahīr Barqūq. It contained about 4,000 books most of which were written by famous authors and calligraphers. The personal collection of Qāḍī Burhānuddīn ibn. Jama'ah was also transferred to it after his death. Up to the 9th Century of the Hij'i era the Mahmūdiah Library was in flourishing condition. On the conquest of Egypt by Ottoman Sultan Salīm-I a greater portion of its collection was transferred to Constantinople. Some books were lost and among others fifty-eight were in the Khadīviah Library at Cairo and six are in the Bankipur

Khuda Bakhsh Library and one in the Library of 'Aligarh Muslim University. Al-Azhar University Library only survived the ravages of the time and its rich collection still reminds one of the glorious days and the love of learning and literature of the Fatimids.

To collect books in libraries attached to mosques and *madrasahs* and to make them available to scholars and students had been the main concern of the founders of the medieval Muslim libraries. Volga Pinto while writing about Muslim libraries observes, "The princes took great care concerning the buildings which were to serve as public libraries. Some of them, like those of Shīrāz, Cordoba and Cairo were placed in separate structures, with many rooms for different use; galleries with shelves in which books were kept, rooms where the visitors could read and study, rooms set apart for those in charge of making copies of manuscripts, rooms which served as literary assemblies, and even in some cases, rooms for musical entertainment, etc. All rooms were richly and comfortably fitted; on the floors were carpets and mats, where the readers in oriental fashion squatted, reading and even writing, holding the sheet of paper or parchment adroitly in the palm of the left hand. The windows and doors were covered with curtains, the chief entrance door having a specially heavy curtain to prevent the cold air from entering".[8] The library of 'Adud al-Dawlah at Shīrāz has been very minutely described by Yāqūt in the following words:

"The library consists of one long vaulted room, annexed to which are store rooms. The prince had made along the large rooms and the store chambers, scaffoldings about the height of a man, three yards wide, of decorated wood which have shelves from top to bottom; the books are arranged on the shelves and for every branch of learning there are separate scaffolds. There are also catalogues in which all the titles of the books are entered. I also saw the ventilation chamber, to which the water is carried by pipes which surround it on every side in circulation". Commenting on Yāqūt's observation Volga Pinto remarks that such arrangement of ventilation led to books being infested by vermin.[9] While describing the library of Mustanṣiriyah College Le Strange observes that the library was arranged in such a manner that any person could have easy access to any book he liked. It was only possible because there was good arrangement of open shelves system.

In the absence of the printing press and the more modern devices of photo-duplicating machines the scribe was an ubiquitarian and he contributed largely to the development of the art of calligraphy. All these libraries briefly mentioned above had a number of scribes on the permanent staff. To publish their works some important authors also engaged scribes. Their services were also required at flourishing book shops.

Some of these copyists were scholars and calligraphers of eminence like Ibn Nadim, the author of *al-Fihrist*, Ibn Sa'd (d. 844), the famous biographer and Yāqūt (d. 1128), the historian and biographer. Yāqūt ibn Adi al-Naṣrānī (d. 974) copied about a hundred pages daily and produced two copies of the commentary of Ṭabarī on the Holy *Qur'ān* in eight volumes, each volume of more than a thousand pages. Abu Bakr al-Daqqāq (d. 1095) made seven copies of *al-Jami'l-Ṣaḥīḥ* of Muslim which was spread over in two volumes in a year.

Before the introduction of paper the cost of a book was very high because of the costly papyrus and parchment used as writing materials. After the introduction of paper in the 8th century books became cheaper than before although they still remained costly because of the human labour and skill involved in publishing this in the absence of the printing press.

Special care was taken for the protection of these costly books using chemicals and having durable bindings. Binding developed into a real art in the hands of the Muslims. Precious books were bound in embossed leather and fragrant wood or thin wooden sheets covered with leather, some inlaid with gold and silver enhancing the face value of the book.[10]

Besides the copyists and binders there were translators and librarians in the staff of the library. Scholarly persons, mostly authors, were employed as librarians of famous libraries. From the data found in the bibliographical dictionaries, it is apparent that most of the scholars served in one or other capacity in libraries as recorded by Gurgis Awad.[11]

Some of the rich collection of the Muslim libraries were, however, destroyed by the Muslims themselves because of the conflict of ideas among Muslim sects, others by invaders, specially Mongols while private collections were destroyed by the owners themselves as Abū Ḥafṣ 'Umar ibn 'Alī known as Ibn al-Mulaqqin (d. 1401) who wrote 300 books, burnt his own collection before his death and Abū Ḥayyān al-Tawḥīdī also burnt his own collection. Caliph al-Ma'mūn's library disappeared after his death for reasons not mentioned by historians. In 1059 the library of Sabur ibn Ardshīr was burnt partly during the great fire at Baghdad set by Sulṭān Tughral Beg, other books were looted and still others were carried off by 'Amid al-Mulk al-Khundūrī. The library of Mustansiriyah college was destroyed by the Mongols in 1258. While Chingiz Khan and Hulāgū burnt libraries and used manuscripts for fuels, Tīmūr collected books during his conquests and built up libraries in his capital at Samarqand.

It was only after conversion to Islām that the Mongols took interest in literary activities and built up libraries. The 'Uthmānlī Turks established libraries in the cities they ruled, Istanbūl thus had fifteen libraries and Constantinople has a rich collection of manuscripts. The National library of Egypt surpassed all the rest of the Muslim libraries in the Middle East.

FOOTNOTES

1. Cf. Meyerhof - *Revista degli studi orientali*, XVII, 1929-30, p. 289.
2. Mawlamal Muhammad Aslam Jajpuri, *Ta'rikh al-Ummat*, Delhi, 1929, VI, 104.
3. Zahid 'Ali, *Ta'rikh Fatimiyin Misr*, vol. II, Karachi, 1963, p. 105.
4. Cf. Volga Pinto, *The Libraries of the Arabs during the time of the Abbasids* in *Islamic Culture*, vol. III, 1929, p. 225; Grahamann, *Bibliotheken*, Vienna, 1926, p. 432.
5. *Kitab al'Asa*, pp. 503-4.
6. Al-Maqrizi, *Khitat*, II, 334; Zahid Ali, I, 224n²; Lane-Poole, p. 131; Pinto, pp. 227-8, 232.3. The Zij prepared during the time of Ma'mun was very much improved by the famous astronomer 'Ali bin Yunus Shasi in the observatory of Hakim.
7. Lane-Poole, pp. 149, 193, Muhammad Zubair, *Islami Kutub Khane*, Delhi, 1961, p. 186.
8. *Islamic Culture*, III, 1929 tr. by Van Kremer.
9. Cf. F. Sarre, *Islamic Book Bindings* (Engl. tr. from German), London, 1923; Dr. Baluch, *Library in Central Asia* in the *Journal of Pakitan Historical Society*, Karachi.
10. *Ancient libraries in Iraq*, Baghdad, 1948.

CHAPTER III

HISPANO

Collection of Books:- The building up of libraries in Muslim Spain[1] began by importing books from the East. As the soldiers landed in Spain, scholars and travellers followed them carrying books along with other valuable products of the East. In the early 8th century the Muslim population of Spain was augmented by a large scale emigration of Syrians and Berbers as well as by the conversion of the serfs and slaves. For the neo-Muslims books on religion and theology and Arabic Grammar had to be imported from the East and were copied to inculcate them in the knowledge of their new religion through the medium of Arabic. During the course of writing the biographical works of men of arts and science 'Arab authors casually mention the import of such books[2] which were among the important articles brought from the East. Among the books on grammar mention may be made of the *Kitab al-Kisa'i* which was brought by the grammarian Judi b. 'Uthman of Mawrur[3] (d. 198/813-4), tutor of the Umayyad prince. The books on jurisprudence of the Maliki schools were introduced into Spain by Abu Zayd b. Dinar (d. 201/816-7).[4] The collection of poems composed by Habib b. Aws read under the direction of the writer and brought to Spain by Ibn al-Muthanna (d. 273/886-7)[5] tutor of 'Abd al-Rahman II and his sons Muhammad and 'Umar. Arabic dictionaries and Arabic works on tradition and poetry were also brought by 'Abd al-Salma al-Khushani (d. 286/899) of Cordova.[6] The *Kitab al-'Ayn*, an Arabic dictionary, was carried from the East by Qasim ibn Thabit of Saragossa.[7] Books on lexicography, poetry and history were brought by Muhammad b. 'Abd Allah al-Ghazi b. QaSys al-Ghazi (died at Tangier about 295/907-8).[8] The books written by 'Ali Muhammad 'Abd Allah b. Muslim ibn Qutaybah and those of 'Amr b. Bahr were introduced by Ahmad b. Muhammad ibn Harun of Baghdad.[9] Many books dealing with the prophetic traditions written by oriental writers including that of Ibn Shaybah were introduced into Spain by Baqi b. Makhlad of Cordova (d. 276/890).[10]

The followers of Maliki School who were patronized by Umayyad rulers, specially Hisham I, did not encourage the import of books dealing with the theological and philosophical ideas other than their own. Still such books were also carried from the East by certain scholars. 'Abd Allah b. Muhammad b. Qasim ibn Hilal of Cordova (d. 272/885-6) brought books dealing with the philosophical ideas of Abu Sulayman Da'ud b. Sulayman. Al-Faradi says that these books became the cause of the spread of the philosophy of Da'ud among the people of Spain.[11] Some other books of heretical nature were brought from Iraq by Ayyub b. Sulayman (d. 326/938) a descendant of Julian (Ilyan).[12]

With the spread of education among the masses, the demand for books increased more and more throughout Muslim Spain specially at Cordova. To meet the pressing demand, the books brought by the highly educated sections of the people were not sufficient. The trade in books, therefore, became very profitable. Like arms, war horses and ornaments for brides, books being exempt from the import duties,[13] the merchant began to take interest in the procurement of books all the more. Among such early travellers and merchants mention may be made of the names of the scholar traveller, Abu Bakr al-Dinawari (d. 349/960),[14] Abu 'Umar b. Yabqi al-Judhami (d. 378/988-0), a merchant of Cordova[15] and Muhammad b. 'Ubayd b. Ayyub (d. 317/929), an artisan of Cordova who manufactured *dibaj* (brocades).[16]

There were also travellers and merchants who built up their own libraries by collecting new and rare books in the East. 'Abd al-Malik b. Habib of Granada,[17] Hashim b. Khalid of Elvira (d. 298/910-11)[18] and Mawhah b. 'Abd al-Qadir of Bajah were notable among them. Mawhah collected a large number of rare works in the East and died in Egypt while returning to Spain. His books were, however, brought to Spain by his family members.[19]

There were also proprietors and teachers of schools who imported books and preserved them in mosques and some private houses to distribute them among students. For example, Harun b. Sabia (d. 238/852-3) of Cordova collected a large number of books in the house of Ahmad b. Khalid.[20]

49

The princes being lovers of art and literature joined with the intelligentsia of Spain in collecting books and importing rare and valuable works from the East. Foremost among them were Abu Sulayam Dahhn (d. after 200/815)[21] and Ibn al-Ahmar al-Hashimi (d. 358/969),[22] who brought books specially on religion. On his return from a long journey through Egypt, 'Iraq and India, Ibn al-Ahmar served in the royal library of the Umayyads and wrote a biographical history of 'Abd al-Rahmn III.[23] Thus by the mutual efforts of the travellers, merchants and princes and above all the intelligentsia of the country many libraries grew up in Spain.

The Royal Library of the Umayyads:– The first library of importance and value in Europe was the royal library of the Umayyads in Cordova. The neo-Muslims' desire for acquiring knowledge gave fresh impetus to the general predeliction of the 'Arabs for reading. In the beginning the movement was slow but it reached its peack with the advent of Hakam II. Himself a litterateur and poet of no mean order, the founder of the Umayyad dynasty, 'Abd al-Rahman I, held periodical literary discourses to which famous men of letters were invited. Among the literary figures of his time mention may be made of Abu al-Mutahashsha[24] the poet, Shaykh Ghazi b. Qays, a great theologian and linguist[25] and Shaykh Abu Musa Hawari, a famous legist.[26] 'Abd al-Rahman's son Hisham I was fond of Arabic poetry and was himself a poet. 'Amr b. 'Abi Ghaffar was the famous poet of his court. Among the learned men, whom Hisham patronized, were 'Isa bin Dinar. 'Abd al-Malik bin Habib, Yahya b. Yaya, [27] Sa'id b. Hasan and Ibn Abu Hind.[28] Hakam I was also a poet[29] and a lover of music and he liked to be surrounded by poets, theologians and litterateurs.[30] Being lovers of learning they established madrasahs and added to the collection of the royal library. The Amirs and Khalifahs, specially 'Abd al-Rahman II and Hakam II, were interested in the collection of books. Their agents travelled through the Eastern towns to collect new and rare books. 'Abbas ibn Nasih the agent of 'Abd al-Rahman II ransacked the bookshops of Mesopotamia to buy Arabic translations of Persian and Greek works on science.[31] The Umayyad library of Cordova became one of the best libraries of the Muslim world during the time of 'Abd al-Rahman II and it was added to and strengthened by 'Abd al-Rahman III. The *Dioscorides* written in golden letters and decorated with beautiful miniature paintings was the first Greek work of importance which was received as a present from the Byzantine emperor, Constantine, by 'Abd al-Rahman the Great. Greek-knowing scholars not being easily available in Spain, the Umayyad Khalifah had to invite Nicolas from Constantinople to translate it into Arabic.[32] The two princes, al-Hakam and Muhammad, receiving good education under the tutorship of native and foreign teachers were not contented with the rich collection of their father 'Abd al-Rahman III and built up their own private libraries. Muhammad and 'Abd al-Rahman died. Hakam united the collections with his own and employed a large staff to reorganize the library and to add more to its collection. The famous grammarian of Jaen al-Rabahi (d. 358/869) who taught Arabic literature at Cordova to many nobles and princes including Mughirah, a brother of Hakam II,[32] the literate and lexicographer of Cordova, Muhammad b. abi al-Husayn al-Fihri of Cordova, and another Arabic scholar Muhammad b. Ma'mar of Jaen[34] were among the famous scholars employed by Hakam II for collection and correction of manuscripts and for copying rare books in his library. Rare and valuable books, old and new, were bought and copied for Hakam II at Alexandria, Cairo, Baghdad and Damascus.[35] Among other famous copyists were Abu'l Fadl b. Harun of Sicily (d. 379/989-90),[36] Yusuf al-Balluti,[37] 'Abbas b. 'Amr of Sicily and Dafar of Baghdad.[38] Female calligraphists also worked in the library of Hakam II. Labna (d. 394/1004 A.C.), secretary to Hakam II[39] and Fatimah (d. 437/1036-7), daughter of Hakam's other secretary Abu Yahya al-Shaballari[40] were known for their beautiful handwriting. The chief librarian of Hakam's library was a high ranking eunuch, Talid, according to whom there were 4,00,000 volumes of books in his royal library. The list of books recording only the names of the authors and titles of the books consisted of 44 volumes of 50 folios each.[41]

Hakam II spent lavishly on the collection of manuscripts. His agents ransacked bookshops and libraries of Baghdad, Damascus, Cairo, Alexandria and other places. Foreign scholars were also employed to collect books for him. Among them mention may be made of the names of Ibn Saban of Egypt, Ibn Ya'qub al-Kindi of Baghdad and Muhammad ibn Farjan.[42] In order to obtain the first copy of the *Kitab al-Aghani*,[43] a history of 'Arab poets and ministerials, composed by Abu'l Faraj al-Aghani, an Umayyad historian and poet of al-'Iraq, al-Hakam sent to the author a thousand dinars. Abu'l Faraj was glad to comply with the order together with a work on the genealogy of the

Umayyads.

Hakam also got books written for his library. Many books were dedicated to him. Among such books was a booklet on the calendar, the *Kitab Awqat al-Sanat* composed by Abu'l-Hasan 'Arib b Sa'id (died towards 370/980-1) of Cordova in 961 A.C. and edited and translated into Latin by Dozy under the title *Calendrier de Cordove de l'annee* 961 in 1873 A.C. The calendar was composed on the model of the Latin Calendar and in the addition of the local Christian Festivals the writer was helped by the bishop Recemundo known as Rabi ben Zeid. The author, who was the secretary to al-Hakam II and perhaps to his father 'Abd al-Rahman III also, wrote some more books, one on astronomy called the *Kitab Tafsil al-Azman wa masalih al-Abdan* and dedicated it to al-Hakam II and two others the *Kitab al-Anwa* (Calendar) and *Surat Yabda' (Simulachre),* which have been exploited fully by ibn al-'Awwam. The fourth work that the author had taken up was the compendium of Tabari, the continuation of the famous chronicle of al-Tabari (d. 310/922-3) and the addition to it of the history of North Africa and Spain. A part of that book has come down to us. This contains important information about the court and the courtiers of 'Abd al-Rahman III.[44] Ibn Mufarraj of Fonteaurea (Cordova) travelled in the East and built up a good library. He wrote many books and dedicated them to Hakam II.[45] Muhammad b. Harth b. Asad al-Khushani of Qayrawan dedicated to him more than a thousand books and booklets, one of which was the *Ta'rikh Qudat al-Qurtubah.*[46] Among other authors who dedicated their works to him were Mutarrif b. 'Isa (d. 377-987/8) of Granada who wrote a history of Elvira,[47] Ibn Faraj of Jaen who composed poems,[48] Muhammad Yusuf of Guadalajara who wrote a geography of Africa.[49] Ibn al-Safar was employed to collect poems referring to the Umayyads of Syria and Spain.[50] 'Arab biographers casually refer to the names of copyists and writers of books preserved in the royal library of Hakam II.[51]

Hakam being a studious scholar went through the important works preserved in his library and made copious notes on the fly leaves which became a source of valuable information for later scholars. Among such books was one, dated 359/970, with a note stating that it was copied for Hakam II which has been recently discovered in Fez by Levi-Provençal.[52]

Contemporary 'Arab scholars have highly spoken of the library of Hakam II, its huge collection and its rare and valuable books. This was, according to them, the biggest collection that a royal library ever possessed in the Medieval world.[53] The spacious original library building failed to accommodate the newly received books. In spite of the employment of a large number of persons, it took six months to remove the rich collection of the library to a new building.[54]

Al-Mansur followed Hakam II and patronized scholars. Among the books dedicated to him were *al-Fusus* written by Sa'id of Baghdad (d. 410-7/1019-1021) who received 5,000 dinars as a gift from Mansur[55] and an illustrated book written by Hasan ibn abi 'Abdah.[56] Abu al-Walid ibn Ma'mar a great historian and paleographist was employed to correct and collate the manuscripts preserved in the library of Mansur and his successors and was entrusted with the work of writing the family history of Banu 'Amir. Later on Mansur being influenced by the 'Ulama was responsible for the burning of a large number of philosophical works in al-Hakam's library.[57] A grim picture of this incident is drawn by Sa'id of Toledo.[58] Describing the pitiful condition of the Cordovans and the peniless situation of the Government, Dozy says that "to obtain a little money Wadih - was even obliged to sell the greater part of Hakam's library."[59] In the beginning of the 11th century during the civil war, the royal library was destroyed and the private libraries of Cordova were plundered. These books of the royal library were sold in the markets of Cordova, Toledo, Seville, Almeria and other cities.[60] Still Cordova continued to be one of the important centres of the arts and science as long as it remained in the hands of the Muslims.

Private Libraries in Cordova:– Kings and princes were, however, not only persons who collected books and built up libraries but people at large also took part in this cultural activity and collected books, sometimes by spending even beyond their means. Among the private libraries of Cordova, the library of Ibn Futays was ranked as the biggest. A very beautiful big library building was constructed by him. It was built in such an ingenious way that all the book-shelves could be seen from one point. Abu 'Abd Allah al-Hadrami (d. 396/1005-6), a learned scholar of Cordova, was employed as librarian as also were six copyists on fixed salaries. The librarian also performed, in addition, the function of an Imam (rector) in the family mosques of

Ibn Futays.[61] The valuable collection of this library was put to auction by his grandsons in the family mosque at Cordova during the civil war.

Even in those hard days it could fetch 40,000 Qasimi dnars.[62] The offer of such a huge amount of money even in the days of the internecine wars indicates the love of books and also importance and popularity of the book market and of the private library of Ibn Futays. Another equally important library and, according to Ibn Abbar, only second to Hakam's library in Cordova was the personal library of Abu al-Walid ibn al-Mawsul (d. 433/1041-2) a great sage of Cordova. He was so fond of reading and writing that he recognised the calligraphy of different copyists and on examining them he was able to name the copyists as well. He was interested in collecting rare and selected books among which were the poetical works from the hands of Abu Ali al-Qali' of Baghdad and works of many other great scribes and calligraphists. After the death of al-Mawsul when his books were sold by his family members they fetched a handsome price, some of the rare books being sold at the rate of eight pages a *mithqal* (dnar).[63] Fatin, a slave of Mansur, recovered a large number of these books after the destruction of the royal library of the Umayyads and built up his own big library of valuable books which were sold at his death.[64] Qasim b. Sa'dan (d. 347/958-9) a great calligraphist and scholar of Rayyuh (Archidona), had a fine private library. Just before his death he made it *waqf* for the use of students and scholars under the supervision of Muhammad b. abi Dulaym.[65] Abu 'Ali al-Ghassani had also an important collection of rare books on various subjects.[66] There were many other scholars who had their personal collections also but did not lend books to others. Al-Juhani of Cordova (d. 395/1004-5) was so much fond of preserving books that he lent them only to those whom he trusted most.[67] It is recorded that there were some others who were forced to dispose of their books for their maintenance. Yahya b. Malika b. 'Ayidh (d. 375/985-6) of Tortosa, a teacher in the Cordova Mosque, travelled in the East for 22 years and wrote a large number of books, was one of them.[68] Even a poor school teacher like Muhammad b. Hazm of Cordova could afford to build up his private collection of valuable books. It is interesting to note that though he was very poorly clad and people were averse to mixing with him socially yet his rich private library attracted many distinguished personalities. This poor but a great scholar died in 282/895-6 while returning from his pilgrimage to

Makkah.[69] Among other important library owners the names of Ibn al-Sabuni (d. 423/1032),[70] Abu Bakr b. Dhakwan (d. 435/1043-4),[71] Ibn 'Awn al-Ma'afiri (d. 512-3/1118-9),[72] and Ibn Mukhtar (d. 535/1140-1)[73] may be mentioned. Ibn Bard of Ecija who lived in Cordova visited the East and brought 18 (camel) loads of books on various subjects.[74]

Public Libraries:– There were several public and mosque libraries in Spain. Ribera contradicts the statement of Casiri which is repeated by later scholars that there had been 70 public libraries in Cordova during the time of Hakam II.[75] According to Ribera there were some mosques in Cordova which had libraries for the use of students otherwise there were all private collections and there was no public library even during the time of Hakam II. From the customs of the common use of mosques and their belongings it is evident that those of mosque libraries to which Ribera refers were used not only by students but also by teachers and worshippers and many others who wanted to use any particular book available in any mosque. Therefore, even if we suppose that there had been no public libraries distinct from the mosque libraries it will be a negation of fact to say that there were no public libraries in Cordova. The mosque libraries were in practice the public libraries. Besides these type of libraries, there were some houses where books were kept for distribution among students to which reference had been made previously.

Muslim Women Scholars:– Ricardo de Beri complains against the lack of culture and education in English women of his days while women of Spain were very much cultured and civilized.[76] Labna, Fatimah, 'Ay'ishah, Radiyah and Khadijah were among the foremost scholars of Spain. On the strength of their education and knowledge Labna and Fatimah held high posts in the court and library of Hakam II. Fatimah, in spite of her old age, wrote books in an elegant and sure hand. While young, she had ransacked the bookshops of Cairo, Damascus and Baghdad in search of rare manuscripts. 'Ay'ishah (d. 400/1009-10) who came of a rich family was a very distinguished poetess of her time and devoted her life to learning. She had a good collection of important and rare manuscripts in her private libary.[77] Radiyah (d. about 423/1032) was the wife of Labib, a noble of the Umayyad court of Cordova. She had also collected a sufficient number of books which later passed on to the hands of Abu

Muhammad b. Khazraj.[78] Ja'far's daughter Khadijah had a library which was inherited by her daughter from Ibn Asad.[79] Women scholars of poor society devoted their life to copying important and valuable books. Ibn al-Fayyad, a historian, says that 170 women were engaged in copying the Qur'an in Kufic character in the eastern suburb of Cordova alone.[80] 'Ay'ishah, daughter of Ahmad, wrote the Qur'an in a very beautiful hand.[81]

Non-Muslim Libraries:– The majority of the Christians living in Muslim Spain adopted manners and customs of the 'Arabs and learnt Arabic and being Arabicized became known as *Musta'rib* (Sp. Mozarabs). Adoption of 'Arab manners and customs was not liked by Alvero of Cordova who complained bitterly against them. He wrote in his book *Indiculus Luminesus* that the young Mozarabs who knew only Arabic built up important libraries of Arabic manuscripts. The Jews did not lag behind the Mozarbs in collecting Arabic books in their private libraries as well as in their synagogues and schools. The leading part was taken by Hasdai b. Shaprut, the court physician of Hakam II.[82] Another Jew, famed for his learning, was Yusuf ibn Isma'il, the minister of Badis b. Habbus of Granada, who had a large collection of Arabic books in his library.[83]

The Cordova Book Market:– Collection of books had become a fairly common national hobby in Muslim Spain and social duty in Cordova. As the drawing room is furnished in these days with valuable and beautiful furniture etc. the house of a nobleman in Cordova was furnished with valuable and rare books written in elegant hands and beautifully bound. The historian Ibn Sa'id heard his father saying that Cordova had been the principal city of book markets because its inhabitants were very much fond of building up the library. He had seen persons without proper education collecting books so that they might claim distinction for their rare manuscripts beautifully written by renowned copyists. Regarding this there is a famous story related by Maqqari. Al-Hadrami a traveller-scholar, visited the book market of Cordova one day and found in a bookshop a work in which he was greatly interested. He tried to purchase it but he could not do so because its price was forced up much higher by another bibliophile. This customer offered an exorbitant price for the book not so much becase he wanted to read it but because he wanted to fill a gap on his bookshelf which had several books of similar binding and ornamentation. This testifies to the Cordovans' love of forming libraries and the keen competition among the buyers of books in the busy market of Cordova. Learned professors, students, skilled copyists and book-sellers flocked from everywhere to Cordova which had become the intellectual centre of the West in the tenth century. Its streets were lined on both sides with long rows of bookshops. The Cordova market had become so famous for the sale of books that sellers and buyers flocked to it from every part of Spain for during the time of Hakam II it had been converted into a great mart of books from every clime and for every taste.[84] Even after the destruction of its royal and private libraries, Cordova, according to Averroes, still possessed in the twelfth century more books than any other city of Spain. While making a comparative study of the importance of Cordova and Seville, Ibn Rushd remarks interestingly that on the death of a learned man in Seville his books were sent to Cordova for sale and also that on the death of a musician in Cordova his instruments were put on sale in Seville.[85]

The fame of the Analusian Muslims in the transciption and binding of books made the Muslim scholars in the East specially Maqdisi to record their achievements.[86] It is stated seventy to eighty thousand volumes of books were copied approximately each year in Cordova along.[87] Ibn Abu al-Fawaris of Cordova copied the Qur'an in a large number by completing two copies a month.[88] The Qur'an copied in the East also passed to Spain and was preserved in mosques. Thus it is known that a quarter of the Qur'an written by the famous Calligraphist Ibn Muqlah was preserved in the mosque of Seville.[89] Caliph 'Uthman's Qur'an was preserved in the Cordova Mosque. It was extant, according to Ibn Bashkuwal, in the mosque until 552/1157 but later was carried by the Muwahhidin to Morocco where it was found preserved in the royal library of Tilimsan in 737/1239. Later it was taken to Portugal and subsequently passed on to a merchant of Fez in 745/1344-5. But according to another version it was burnt along with other copies of the Qur'an of the Cordova Mosque by the Christians when they occupied the city during the time of Ibn Hamdun.[90] Recent infromation is of its preservation in Istanbul discussed elsewhere by the present writer.

Provincial Libraries:– Till the tenth century provincial libraries did not rise much to importance, though literary activities continued in those places also while Cordova remained the centre of culture and civilization. After the fall of this city the centre of civilization shifted elsewhere and petty dynasties vied each other..

Seville and Badajoz:– Among the Muluk al-Tawa'if, the 'Abbadids of Seville had an important royal library. Seville did not stand in comparison to Cordova in the matter of having rich and valuable libraries and bookshops but it was decidedly better in that regard than any other town of Spain. Ibn al-Khatib of Granada mentions frequently the books written in Seville which distinguished it from the rest of Spain.[91] Ibn al-Abbar speaks of the street lined on both sides by bookshops, in one of which he came upon a rare copy of *Ibn Muzayn,* a short history of Razi.[92] Ibn Sarah al-Bakri, a poet of Santaren, earned his livelihood by copying books in Seville.[93] The copyist Abu Zayd al-Judhami of Seville is known to have settled himself at Cordova.[94]

Among the great bibliophiles of Seville were Sharf al-Dawlah, son of the 'Abbadid ruler al-Mu'tamid,[95] Ibn al-Ahdab (d. 437/1045-6),[96] Abu Bakr ibn al.'Arabi,[97] Muhammad ibn Khayr and Ibn Marwan al-Baji. The valuable collection of the library of Muhammad ibn Khayr was sold after his death[98] and Abu Marwan endowed his own library to the Qadi of the mosque of Seville, Ibn al-Hajjaj al-Lakhmi (d. 601/1204-5).[99]

Abu Muzaffar b. al-Aftas of Badajoz had such a valuable and comprehensive library from which he collected all the requisite materials for the compilation of his famous book *al-Muzaffriyah* an encyclopaedic work in fifty volumes dealing with the art of war, politics, history, fables and other branches of the sciences and the arts.[100]

Northern Towns:– Among the important towns of the North, Toledo and Saragossa were in the possession of the Muslims for long. The Gothic capital, Toledo, was still an important town during the time of the Umayyads. During the civil war the library of Hakam II was plundered and books were sold in the markets of Toledo to which the European students flocked for the study of Oriental arts and sciences. The Banu Dhu al-Nun rulers of Toledo had their own royal library. Books of many private libraries found their way there. Among the private libraries the rich collection of Ibn Maymun which was saved from fire when it broke out in the markets of Toledo,[101] and those of

Abu 'Amir ibn Ibrahim (d. 523/1129)[102] and Abu Muhammad ibn al-Hilali (d. 458/1066)[103] were important. Among other libraries were those of the calligraphists, Ibn al-Shaykh (d. 440/1048-9),[104] Ibn al-Khattar (d. 438/1046-7),[105] Ibn Hatim al-Tamimi (d. 469/1076-7)[106] and Abu al-Walid ibn al-Hanshi who had imported many important works from the East to enrich his collection.[107]

Saragossa being the farthest limit of the Muslim possession in the North-East of Spain had always been the battle-ground for the two rival communities, the Muslims and the Christians. Muslim scholars had always to migrate from there to the South. In spite of the horrible scenes of war, the Banu Hud rulers of Saragossa did patronize learned men, especially philosophers. Geometricians like al-Muqtadir and physicians like Ibn Buklaris the author of *al-Mustayni*, a famous work of materia medica dedicated to al-Mustayn, flourished in Saragossa.[108] Ibn Sandur b. Mantil (d. before 500/1106-7) was another important bibliophile of Saragossa.[109] Finally when it was conquered by Alfonso I, these collectors of books migrated from Saragossa and Calatayud to the South.[110] Ibn Matruh and Ibn Saghir the famous book-seller and the bibliophile of Saragossa migrated to Valencia.

Eastern Towns:- The emigrant scholars and book-sellers from Saragossa, Calatayud and other cities of Aragon took refuge in - Valencia. Among such refugees were Ibn Matruh[111] and Ibn al-Saghir, whose son Ahmad was honoured by the appointment as a librarian in the royal library of the Muwahhidin[112] who have been mentioned above and also Ibn Sidray (d. 548/1153-4) the book-seller of Calatayud.[113]

Among the famous bibliophiles of Valencia were 'Abd Allah al-Marrawshi (d. 487/1094) two-thirds of whose books i.e., 143 loads were transported to the palace of Ibn Dinun, the king of Valencia,[114] 'Ali b. Hudhayl (d. 564/1168-9) who inherited a big library from his step-father, Abu Da'ud al-Maqqari,[115] Ibn 'Ayshun al.Ma'afiri (d. 547/1178-9) who collected a large number of books and constructed a mosque in his name near the Alcantara Gate of Valencia.[116]
Many of the book-sellers of Valencia migrated to other towns of the Levant. Ibn S'adat of Murcia (d. 566/1170-1) whose ancestors were of Valencia flourished in Jativa and inherited a very rich library.[117] The

botanist Ibn al-Rumia of Jativa who was a follower of Ibn Hazm of Cordova spent lavishly on the collection of rare books for his library.[118] Ibn al-Faras of Granada (d. 567/1171-2) gave up his political activities which he had at Cordova and Valencia and settled down at Murcia. He dedicated his life to literary activities and made a very excellent collection of manuscripts.[119]

Almeria was another seat of culture in the East. Abu Ja'far b. 'Abbas, prime minister of Zuhayr of Almeria, was an excellent calligraphist and possessed great riches of which he spent 5,00,000 *mithqals* (Ja'fari gold dinar) on the purchase of books, sometimes paying three times the usual price for them. Thus he built up a grand library containing 4,00,000 volumes of books, besides innumerable papers and leaflets.[120] The Qadi of Almeria, 'Abd al-Haq ibn 'Atiyah, was a great book-collector.[121] Maymun ibn Yasin (d. 530/1135-6) a Berber of the Sanhajah tribe of Almeria was a famous book-seller[122] and Nasr of Almeria a renowned scribe.[123]

Malaga also produced men of arts and science. Ibn Mufassal of Malaga made seventy copies of the Qur'an and wrote many other works.[124] Ibn Lope had a famous collection of books which he made over to the chief mosque of Malaga.[125] Ibn Madrak al-Ghassani,[126] and 'Uthamn ibn Mandur[127] were famous calligraphists and book-sellers. 'Isa of Ronda had built up a good collection of books by importing them from the East but he subsequently lost them.[128] Muhammad ibn al-Hakim al-Lakhmi of Ronda orginally hailed from Seville had built up a valuable collection of books.[129]

The Nasird kingdom of Granada became the refuge of the Muslims who had emigrated from other Muslim zones which were gradually reconquered by the Christians of the North. As a result, the number of book-sellers and bibliophiles increased considerably in Granada and it was a remarkable fact that the refugees possessed much more literary treasures than the natives of Granada. The Nasrid rulers of Granada patronized scholars and showed interest in building up library. The royal library possessed rare and valuable manuscripts dealing with numerous subjects. There were private libraries, among which those of the great artist Ibn Farsun,[130] Abu'l Qasim al-Qalbi, the teacher of Ibn al-Khatib[131] and Abu 'Abd 'Allah Ataraz[132] were important and held large numbers of rare manuscripts. Al-Zubaydi, a famous scholar of Jaen, settled at Granada and built up a good library specially by himself writing and copying books. His library was plundered by the Esquilula.[133] Ibn Sarah of Santaren[134] and Aben Socral[135] were famous calligraphists and Ibn Ballis of Granada a great book-seller.[136]

Poets, historians, jurists, geographers, astronomers, botanists, chemists and calligraphists enjoyed the confidence of the Nasird rulers and were on intimate terms with them. Among the favourite subjects with the Spanish 'Arabs were poetry, fictions, lexicography, history, philosophy, jurisprudence, law of contracts, *hisbah* rules and regulations of municipality and markets, geography, cartography, astronomy, mathematics, botany and chemistry on which they had written widely and had also collected books on these exhaustively in their libraries.

Destruction of Arabic Manuscripts:– From the above mentioned accounts it is clear how Arabic learning was widely spread and profusely infused in Muslim Spain leading to the growth of many libraries in the chief cities such as Cordova, Toledo, Seville and Granada. Gradually with the loss of political power and the fall of Muslim cities into Christian hands, the Muslims receded more and more to the South till they took refuge in Granada. But with the fall of their last stronghold, Granada, also their life and property, infact, everything they possessed, their language, literature and culture were all left at the mercy of the victorious Christians who did not prove as tolerant towards their Muslim subjects as the Muslims had been to the Christians and the Jews. The victorious Christians went against the terms of the capitulation of Granada[137] and persecuted their Muslim subjects called the Moriscos because they spoke and wrote Arabic and professed Islam a religion other than the State religion of Christianity. Muslims' schools were closed, libraries were burnt down and repressive laws were passed to compel them to renounce the Arabic language. 'Arab manners and customs and most of the Moriscos were ultimately forced to accept Christianity. But when the persuasion and force failed to convert some to Christianity, they were violently expelled from the country.

These Christians, however, had not been so very intolerant when the Muslims had been in power as they had become after the Muslims surrendered Granada. In the twelfth and thirteenth centuries, schools and universities had been founded by the Christians in important towns to translate Arabic books into Latin and to impart 'Arabic-Latin education. The names of the Arabic-Latin schools of Toledo and Seville, and of the universities of Palencia, Salamanca and Lerida may be mentioned in this connection.[138] Many works on science, arts and philosophy, were translated from Arabic into Latin and Romance. Towards the close of the fifteenth century, all patronage to Arabic language and literature was withdrawn and within eight years after the fall of Granada a regime of coersion and torture began in violation of the terms of capitulation. The collections in the Muslim libraries of Granada, except works dealing with philosophy, medicine and history, were taken to the plaza of Bibarrambla and burnt at the order of El Cardinal Ximines de Cisneros, the priest-in-charge of the conversion of Muslims to Christianity, in 1499 A.C. "He wished," says Nicholson "to annihilate the record of seven centuries of Muhammadan culture in a single day."[139]

A contemporary journalist who did not know Arabic and had himself not lost any book as a result of the fire puts the figure of the Arabic works destroyed at 2,000,000 (two millions).[140] According to Ribera, who wrote a biography of Cardinal Ximines, the number of Arabic manuscripts consumed was one million and five thousand.[141] The impartial view of the journalist mentioned above has been contradicted by another biographer of Ximines, Simonet, by observing that Muslims were uncivilized and their libraries did not possess such a large number of books.[142] This is simply a negation of the fact. In spite of his partiality, even Ribera admits that the Muslms of Spain were very highly civilized, even more than their brethren in the East, and that their libraries at Granada were rich enough to have possessed two million books.[143]

After the fall of Granada neither were Arabic books imported nor written within the country; rather, the old collection of Arabic manuscripts when and wherever found were destroyed. In spite of the losses caused by time, humidity and the corrosine nature of the materials utilized for writing purposes, a large number of the books in their collection would have been extant today had they not been set on fire and destroyed by the Christians, or buried and hidden under rocks by the Moriscos themselves or alternatively taken out of the country by the latter at the time of their expulsion.

There is not much point in recording the losses of books caused in transit or books exported to foreign countries because one was unavoidable and another brought foreign goods of equal value. Still for the satisfactrion of the critics they are mentioned below. In importing books from the East, the entire collection of Abu Musa al-Hawwari who worked as Qadi at Ecija during the time of 'Abd al-Rahman II,[144] Abu Yahya of Cordova (d. 385/995)[145] and Ibn Hawt Allah of Onda (d. 612/1215-6)[146] were lost in transit.

The export of books was much less in value than that of their import. 'Atiyah b. Sa'id (d. about 408/1017-8) a bibliophile of Spain carried many camel loads of books to the East.[147] The biographer al-humaydi distributed his collections among the learned men of the East[148] and Abu Bakr b. Yasir (d. 563/1167-8) of Jaen, the librarian of the library of one Nur al-Din, among the students and traditionists of the East.[149] A considerable number of books wer exported to North Africa. In the beginning of the eleventh century, many scholars of Spain went to Fez and settled there.[150] The students of Morocco studying in Spain on their return journey carried a large number of books from Spain. Yasaltan b. Da'ud of Aghmat (d. 372/982-3)[151] and Muhammad b. 'Abd al-Haq of Tilimsan (d. 625/1228)[152] studied in Spain and carried books to their country. Ibn Maljum (d. 535/1140-1) of Morocco was another student who studied in Spain and built up a very excellent library which was sold by his son for 4,000 dinars.[153] Keeping in view the necessity of conserving the books to foreign countries was not at all a loss to Spain. The migration of scholars along with their valuable collections, some being irreplaceable, is a matter really to be taken into consideration especially so when the expelled Moriscos carried to North Africa and the East important and rare works like those of the philosopher Ibn 'Arabi, grammarian Ibn Malik, politician Abu Bakr of Tortosa, theologian Ibn Farru of Jativa, poet Ibn Khaja of Alcira, Ibn Khaqan and others.[154]

Another loss which was actually more serious in nature was that caused by the burning of philosophical works in Muslim Spain. Philosophers holding other than Maliki ideas were not tolerated, they were maltreated and their books were burnt unofficially. Ibn Masarrah (883-931)[155] was tortured and the philosophical works of the library of Ibn Kulayb was burnt at the instigation of Maliki theologians.[156] This intolerance was, however, not approved of by the

State and the culprits were taken to task. Hakam II patronized the philosophers of all schools but Hajib al Mansur the Prime Minister of Hisham II, was overpowered by the theologians and had to destroy a section of Hakam's library containing works on philosophy.[157] Books of heretical contents and doubtful nature were searched for in the markets and libraries and were burnt by the orthodox Malikis. The library of Ibn Hazm met the same fate.[158] After the arrival of the Murabitun the practice of burning philosophical works and books of heretical contents including scholastic theology became more and more common and was often carried out with the sanction of the state. Abu Ishaq b. Tashufin sacked many libraries like that of Abu Bakr b. Abi Laylaha, a great scholar of Murcia (d. 566/1170-1) and carried the books to Morocco.[159] The Muwahhidun who believed in scholastic and philosophical ideas in the beginning ordered the collection of the theological works of Maliki sect and carried them to Fez where they were burnt.[160] The works of Muhammad Abu Bakr (d. 599/1202-3) were burnt at the order of the Sultan (about 580/1184-5.)[161] This enraged the Andalusian Muslims who began to call the Mawahhidun heretics. In order to appease them the Muwahhidun went against the philosophers Averroes and Ibn Tufayl and others, whom they had patronized so long, and persecuted them and destroyed their books by setting fire.[162] The collection of scientific works of Abu al-Hajjaj al-Marini of Seville suffered at the hands of the Muwahiddin.[163]

The Muwahiddun employed Spanish calligraphists in their library in Morocco. The librarian of their royal library was also a Spanish Abu al-'Abbas b. Asawira of Valencia.[164]

In spite of all these casual losses, specially of the philsophical and scholastic works enumerated shortly above, there had been a large stock of books at Granada in the fifteenth century both in the royal library and in other private libraries. These huge collections of Arabic manuscripts in the possession of Moriscos living in Valencia, Aragon and other parts of Spain, suffered losses at the hands of the Christians. Among the books destroyed at Bibarrambla there were manuscripts elegantly written and beautifully decorated with many plates and book-clasps of silver and gold encrusted with pearls of the value of more than 10,000 ducats according to an account of Padre Alcolea.[165] Even after this, the destruction of their Arabic manuscripts continued. This practice of burning Arabic works was later legalised by passing laws. In 1511 A.C. Dona Juana passed an order for the burining of Arabic books on religion. Accordingly Moriscos were ordered to present their Arabic manuscripts for the examination and scrutiny of their contents. The books on Islamic laws and religion were thus separated from the others and burnt. Since then the *Santo oficio* began to take drastic steps against those who yet retained Arabic manuscripts on the *Qur'an, Hadith* and *Fiqah* and such books were also collected and burnt. Even at the risk of their lives the Moriscos tried to hide such books and ultimately, at the time of their final expulsion, they had to leave behind some of these books in their houses as reported by Fray Marcos de Guadalajara.[166] There is preserved an Arabic manuscript of a grammer in the university library of Valencia with the note, "I, Jamie Ferrando, found this book in a village, Laguar, after the Moors had climbed up the hill (for safety), in the house of Mil-Leni de Guatest, the chief of the Moors, and as it is written in Arabic letters I have not met a man who could read it. I am afraid it may be a copy of the Qur'an of Muhammad."[167] In August 1584, the alcalde of Altea compelled the nephew of Junca, an *alfaqui* of the Moriscos, to deposit a sack full of the copies of the *Qur'an* with the Santo Oficio.[168] Even after the expulsion of the Moriscos burning of Arabic manuscripts continued in full swing and in course of time the burning of Arabic manuscripts became an annual festival.[169] This was celebrated until quite recently in memory of the Bibarrambla bonfire mentioned above as a plan of contempt for Islam and its teaching.

Considering that the preservation of Arabic books was pernicious and injurious to the Christian religion and their society, the bishop burnt them and from time to time the Christian kings passed orders for their destruction but sometimes gave them away as presents to neighbouring Muslim kings. Sancho IV entered into friendly relations with the Banu Marins and presented them three loads of important books.[170]. Ribera says, "But the books which they (Muslims) left unburnt and were preserved in the hands of Christians, Jews and Moriscos, we lost, sometimes by giving as presents as it happened during the time of Sancho IV and at other times by burning them, thus we have not been less unscrupulous than the Muslims themselves, whose example, in this respect, we merely imitated". In making such a statement, he has failed to remain impartial and tried to defend the Christians against the stain on their record which they had incurred in the opinion of scholars.

Conclusion:- From the historians and biographers's accounts of libraries, inadequate though they are, the following facts may be deduced for the information of persons interested in library of science.

That the Medieval Muslims were well aware of the needs of library and accordingly had library buildings constructed providing rooms for stacks, copyists, binders, cataloguers and librarians, readers and lecturers in such a way that the whole library was visible from one central point.

That in Muslim Spain there were private and public libraries in the building which men and women, masters and slaves, kings and people, scholars and laymen all worked alike indicating the high standard of literacy and culture in Muslim Spain.

That these books arranged on the shelves subjectwise with a catalogue for the ready reference by scholars and students.

That new and original works were written, valuable Greek and Latin works were translated into Arabic and rare and important Arabic books were transcribed by expert calligraphists for the wide circulation of new ideas and discoveries. In the absence of the printing machine, the scribes rendered their services for the wide spread of knowledge. In spite of the fact that transcription was a very costly affair, books were freely bought and sold in the book markets of Spain.

That special care was taken to preserve those costly books by binding them in embossed leather and fragrant wood. Their value was increased further by inlaying them with gold and silver lettering and ornamentation.

The persons of great learning and culture were employed to run the administration of the libraries.

That due to the conflict of ideas among different Muslim sects a considerable number of books were destroyed by Muslims themselves but still there were million of books in the libraries of Granada when it was surrendered to the Christians who rejoiced in burning valuable collections of Muslim libraries.

II - ARABIC MANUSCRIPTS IN MODERN SPANISH LIBRARIES

During the period of about 800 years of Muslim rule in Spain the material and cultural improvements that the Muslims made were substantial and far-reaching. They carried literary treasures from the East to Spain, translated Greek and Latin works into Arabic, wrote new and important books, transcribed rare and valuable manuscripts and preserved them in private and public libraries. Those works dealt with various subjects like poetry, philosophy, fiction, lexicography, history, jurisprudence, law of contracts, *hisbah* (rules and regulations of municipalities and markets), geography, astronomy, mathematics, botany and chemistry.

The political and religious rivalry which prevailed between Christians and Muslims did not, however affect their cultural contact. With every fresh reconquest of the Muslim territory in Spain, the Christians acquired new treasures in the shape of books whose study was encouraged by the Christian kings. There were more commentaries than translations of Greek originals in the libraries of Muslim Spain which gradually came into the hands of the Christians.

In Cordova the Arabic school of translation was started by 'Abd al-Rahman II and many Greek scientific and philosphical works were translated into Arabic while others were imported from the East. The Christians were not mere spectators but they also copied the Muslims in their cultural activity. Schools and universities were founded in important towns to translate Arabic books into Latin and to impart 'Arabic-Latin education to Christian youths. The Arabic-Latin schools of Teledo and Seville and the universities of Palencia, Salamanca and Lerida grew to importance. Raimundo, the Archbishop of Toledo (1125-52 A.C.), started a school of translation at Toledo which played a great part in transmitting the Eastern learning to the West. Another Arabic-Latin school was opened at Seville by Alfonse X in 1215. Much later another university was founded at Lerida by Jaime II in 1300. All these institutions served to impart Arabic learning and translate Arabic works on various subjects into Latin and the Romance languages. Just as systematic translations had once brought home the ancient science of the Greeks to the 'Arabs, so now the medieval West, by the very same method of translation, acquired knowledge of the sciences of the 'Arabs.

Due to the conflict of ideas among the different Muslim sects a considerable number of books had been destroyed by the Muslims themselves but still there were millions of books in the libraries of Granada when it was surrendered to the Christians who rejoiced in burning valuable collections of the Muslim libraries. Towards the close of the fifteenth century all patronage to Arabic language and literature was withdrawn by the Christians and within eight years after the fall of Granada a regime of coercion and torture began in violation of the terms of capitulation. About two million Arabic manuscripts were destroyed by fire in the plaza of Bibarrambla (Granada) at the order of El Cardinal Jimines de Cisneros, the priest-in-charge of the conversion of Muslims to Christianity, in 1499 A.C. This vandalism and further destruction of Arabic manuscripts have made them extremely scarce in Spain; later on, however, some Christian noble minds realised the importance of this form of the national treasure and began to preserve it in different libraries such as the Escurial Library and the National Library of Madrid.

The Escurial Library:- The famous library of the Escurial is housed in the Escurial the foundation stone of which was laid by Philip II in commemoration of his victory over France and as a reparation of the destruction of the Convent St. Lawrence at Quentin in France. The work was started under the supervision of two architects, Juan Bautista de Toledo and Juan de Herrera, in April 1563. It was completed in September 1584. Around the monastery a small city grew up. It has become the summer residence for the people of Madrid. Philip II opened the library of the Escurial in 1575 A.C. with 4,000 volumes of his own private collection. Since then private collections of the clergy, chiefs and scholars were added to this library assisting it to develop gradually. During the time of Philip III, the collection was augmented considerably, particularly by the addition of 4,000 Arabic manuscripts of the library of Muley Zidan, the Muslim ruler of Morocco.

While the Spaniards and the North Africans were at war towards the last quarter of the fifteenth century, two vessels carrying 3,980 Arabic manuscripts[1] belonging to Muley Zidan were captured by Pedro de Lara near Zale at a short distance from the port of Mamora. After negotiating with the Spanish King, Muley Zidan agreed to offer a big quantity of gold and silver and to free the Christian prisoners of war on condition that the books would be returned to him. But before the actual exchange of books took place and indemnities given, Muley Zidan's nephew, Muley 'Abd Allah, rebelled and the former became entangled in civil war and Philip ordered the restoration and preservation of these manuscripts in the monastery of St. Lawrence.[2] Speaking about this negotiation, Ribera says that when Muley Zidan negotiated with the Spanish King for the return of the books, the Inquisitor General was consulted. He advised the Spanish king to retain the manuscripts relating to Muslim religion as security for the good conduct of the Emperor of Morocco and to return to him books only on astrology, medicine, mathematics, history and such other subjects. The Council of State, however, considered the opinion of the Inquisitor being too much generous, resolved to burn all of them although there were a few members who opined that only books dealing with religion should be destroyed. The Marques of Velada, however, intervened and advised the Monarch to preserve this unique collection of Arabic manuscripts in safe custody and this counsel was accepted by the king.[3]

Philip III was requested to deposit the banned Arabic manuscripts then lying with a servant of Juan Idiaquez and others, in the Monastery along with the other Arabic manuscripts in the Escurial Library. Francisco de Guarmendi after scrutinizing the title and contents of the manuscripts submitted a report to the Emperor saying that about 2,000 manuscripts were copies of the Qur'an and its commentaries and 2,000 manuscripts were on various other subjects including philosophy, mathematics and medicine, and suggested to him that the prohibited manuscripts should be kept separately.[4] In 1621, the Emperor, Philip III, ordered Guarmendi to put them on shelves in the Royal Library of the Escurial and informed Juan Peralta, the rector of San Lorenzo, accordingly and prohibited him from mixing up the lot of banned manuscripts with others without an order from the Emperor.[5]

In 1651, Muley Muhammad, son of Muley Zidan, sent a delegation with the Chief Fr. Pedro de Alcantara, the guardian of the convent of Franciscanos descalzos of Morocco, to Philip IV to persuade the Emperor to return the collection of manuscripts. This time also the members of the Council of State and the Inquisition were divided in their opinion. Many were of the opinion that the copies of the Qur'an should be burnt and the rest might be returned, while some others were of the opinion that except the copies of the *Qur'an* and *Hadith* the manuscripts might be returned and a few absolute in minority were of the opinion that the whole lot might be returned to the ruler of Morocco. However, the negotiation failed and the books were not returned.[6]

Throughout the sixteenth and seventeenth centuries, the Muslim Emperors of Morocco negotiated for the return of the books but the Christian rulers neither returned the books nor made any use of these valuable sources of Muslim cultural history of the West. Half of these books, which were left uncared for, were ravaged by a disastrous fire in 1671 A.C. This year the library caught fire and more than 5,000 volumes including 2,000 Arabic manuscripts were consumed. During the napoleonic invasion and the peninsular war of resistance when the library was removed to Madrid a large number of works were lost. Between 1820 and 1823, further losses to the rich collection of the library occurred. In spite of all these losses, the Escurial libary is, however, today one of the finest libraries in the world and possesses a total number of 44,742 volumes, 40,000 being printed books, 2,000 Arabic manuscripts, 2,090 manuscripts in Latin and Spanish languages, 580 Greek manuscripts and 72 Hebrew manuscripts.[7] *The Kitab Akriyat al-Sufun*[8] of Abu'l Qasim Khalaf b. Afras, *The Kitab al-Naffaq* of 'Umar b. Rashiq and the *Kitab Munafa' al-Haywan* of 'Ali b. Muhammad b. 'Abd al-'Aziz (d. 762/1360-1) are among the important unpublished manuscripts of the library. The first book deals with the hiring of boats, the second with the marriage contract and the responsbilities of the husband for the maintenance of his wife and the third with the history of animals, birds and other creatures illustrated by miniature paintings. The catalogue of Arabic manuscripts was prepared in Latin by Casiri and published in two volumes in 1760-70 A.C. A more scientific catalogue was prepared later in French by Hartwig Derenbourge and Levi Provencal in three volumes. A further catalogue of 448 Arabic manuscripts, preserved in the Escurial Library, was prepared by D. Nemesio Morata and published in *Al-Andalus*, II, pp. 87-182.

The main hall of the library is spacious with beautifully painted murals. The ceiling was painted in fresco by the famous Spanish artist Tibaldi. Some articles of interest along with books written elegantly in golden letters are kept here on exhibition. There are seven glass show-cases in the middle of the hall and in the second of these there are exhibited a copy of Bible translated in Hebrew in the fifteenth century, a copy of the Qur'an belonging to Muley Zidan the above mentioned sixteenth century Arabic manuscript dealing with the history of animals and also several other Arabic and Persian manuscripts. They are all beautifully written in golden letters. These books which are on exhibition can only be consulted by scholars, with special permission from the authorities of Madrid.

Besides the monastery, the Prince's lodge *(Casita del Principe)* is a building in the Escurial which is worth seeing. The University of the Escurial, though a private organization, is renowned for its Faculty of Law. The school of the Escurial, known as *Seminario*, is functioning from the time of Philip II and teaches theology, philosophy and the liberal arts.

Libraries in Madrid:- The Medieval City of Cordova has lost its previous importance and the cultural activities shifted from there to Madrid originally founded by the 'Arabs under the name *'Marjit'*. In Madrid there are several libraries and institutions which are known for the collection of Arabic manuscripts, the National Library of Madrid[9] being the most important of them all.

In the beginning of the seventeenth century the Royal Library of Spain was known as Library of the 'Reina Madre'. It contained numerous important books and manuscripts and was housed in the tower of the Alcazar. Philip V added valuable collections of books written in foreign languages which were brought from France. The Royal Library containing 8,000 books was for the first time opened to the public on the 1st March 1712. A few months later, the personal collection of the Archbishop of Valencia was added to it. Later on the Royal Museum containing coins and mathematical instruments was also attached to it. P. Robinet was appointed as the first director and Gabriel Alvarez de Toledo as the first librarian. During the period of the French domination under Napoleon, the library suffered greatly and books were used for making cartridges and within ten years 1809-1819, the books were removed twice, first from the royal palace to the convent of the Trinity and again from there to the palace of Almirantazgo.

In 1836, it was declared as the National Library of Madrid and two years later rules and regulations were framed for the preservation of its books. Works of objectionable nature including those of the Moors and the Moriscos were placed in one room and were not issued to the readers without the permission of the Pope.

The site of the National Library and Museum building was selected in Paeo de Recoletes and the foundation-stone was laid on the 21st April, 1866. It took twenty-six years to complete this grand building. The library containing 500,000 volumes including 9,000 rare books and manuscripts was transfered to this building in 1894 A.C. After 1,900 the private collection of Pascual de Gayangos was added to this. Catalogues of manuscripts and books were prepared under the supervision of Marcelino Menendez Pelayo.

In the annual exhibitions rare books, important manuscripts and curious articles were displayed to attract the people. In such exhbitions, particularly those of the Historical Exhibition of America (Jan., 1891), the works of Don Quijote (1902), the third century anniversary of the death of Cervantes (23rd April, 1914) and the fourth century anniversary of the birth of the great Portuguese epic poet, Luis de Gamoens (13th December, 1924) are important and famous. The art of the exhibition of books has reached such a height that the exhibitions impart considerable cultural educations among the people in a very striking manner. The December, 1955, exhibition of books at the National Library was arranged in such a way that it illustrated a gradual process of the development of Latin calligraphy, introduction and development of paper manufacture and printing and binding of book II.

In April, 1918, the sections archives, library and archeology were re-organised and given new impetus. In 1930, a large number of books in foreign language were added to the already rich collection of the library with the idea of making it one of the most famous libraries of the world. The library suffered from ravages of civil war in 1936-1939.

Among the important sections of the Library are of Lope de Vega, Cervantes, Goya and of the manuscripts and rare books section. There are more than 30,000 rare books among which is also a copy of the *Dioscorides* copied by Anvers Juan Latio in 1555. This is a Greek work on plants and medicines, a copy of which had been received first in Spain by 'Abd al-Rahman III of Cordova as a present from Constantine the Greek Emperor of Byzantium.

The printing press was introduced into Spain for the first time by A. Juan Gensfleisch known as Gutenberg and the first book was printed in Spain between 1436 and 1438. However, incunabula printed before 1457 are neither dated nor do they bear the names of their printers and publishers. The earliest dated incunabula is Johnnes de (Balbi, Giovanni), Catholicon Maguntiae (J. Gutenberg) dated 1460, in 373 folios.

Many old works of engraving, lithography, etc., are preserved in a section of the Fine Arts. They are not so important from the artistic point of view as from the historical point of view. There are about 200,000 engraved works and 10,000 original pictures and drawings representing the styles of different artistis of various periods. These pictures drawn by natives as well as foreigners illuminate all stages of the lives of picturesque figures such as warriors and literary personages.

Out of about 25,000 volumes in the manuscript section 500 are autographs of foreign as well as of native scholars. The catalogue of Arabic manuscripts was prepared by F. Guillen Robles at Madrid in 1889. Some more important Arabic manuscripts have been added later. Among the important unpublished Arabic manuscripts held by the library are:-

Ibn abi Zamanin's (d. 1007-8 A.C.) the *Muntakhab al-Ahkam*[11] on judicial edicts — folio 108, maghribi letter. Another incomplete manuscript of the same work in 28 folios is also there — maghribi letter.

Abu'l Qasim Salmun al-Qinini's *al-'Iqd al-Munazzam lil Hukkam fima yajra bayn Aydihim min al-Wa tha'iq wa'l Ahkam*[12] also a collection of judicial laws.

There are also various documents of the Moriscos.

Among the works written by Christian authors in the tenth and eleventh centuries are:-

Morales de San Gregorio el Magno, *A Visigothic letter of the Year* 945, folios 502 written on parchment and calf skin — with Visigothic miniature paintings.

Etimologias of San Isidora, tenth century, folios, 163, written on parchment with coloured geometrical figures.

The degrees of a religious council, collected by the Abbot Superino, tenth century, folios 345, written on parchment with miniatures of Byzantine styles.

Fuero Juzgo, *The Year* 1058, folios 186, written on *pergamena* with epigraphs and marginal decorations in red and blue of Mozarab style.

The Commentaries of the Apocalypse of San Juan by San Beato of Liebana, copied by Facundus in 1047, possessed by the King Fernando and Queen Sancha, folios 316, written on calf skin with more than 100 miniatures of the Mozarabs.

The Sacred Bible of Avilab written in Italian Carolingian small letters towards the end of the eleventh century and in French in the beginning of the twelfth century.

Among rare and curious bindings are one of the eighteenth century in red velvet with the royal shield embroidered with gold and silk on both sides of the binding and another mudejar with lining in velvet ornamented with gold lace, initials of the Catholic kings, crowns and brooches of Moorish enamel and engraved silver cover with the figure of San Miguel.

There are four other libraries in Madrid which are known for the collection of Arabic manuscripts and books and study of Hispano-

Arab culture in Spain. The Library of the Institute of Miguel Asin Madrid (School of Arabic Studies) and that of the Royal Academy of History are the foremost among them. Besides having a large number of published Arabic works, they possess some rare and important manuscripts especially on contracts and sale-deeds. Among the other rare manuscripts the Miguel Asin Institute possesses a copy of the collection of the *risalahs* of Ibn Hazm of Cordova (11th century),[13] *al-Sifr al-Thani min al-Watha'iq wa al-Masa'il al-Majmua'h*[14] of 'Abd Allah b. Futah of Alpuente (Valencia) and *al-Maqsad al.Mahmud fi Talkhis al-'Uqud*[15] of Abu al-Hasan of Algeciras. An incomplete manuscript of *al-Muqna' fi 'Ilm al-Shurut*[16] of Ahmad ibn Mughith of Toledo (d. 459/1067) on contracts is preserved among other rare works under the title *al-Watha'iq Musta'mal* copied by Sulayman Muhammad b. al-Khazanji in the Gayangos collection of Arabic manuscripts at the Academy of History. The Egyptian Institute of Madrid and the Hispano-Arab Institute of Madrid are the other two institutions which have been established with the idea of conducting researches in Hispano-Arab culture. Their libraries also have valuable collections. The first Director of the Hispano-Arab Institute was the learned Arabic scholar, Don Emilio Gari Gomez. The University of Madrid has a chair of Arabic but its library was poor as far as Arabic books and manuscripts are concerned as observed by me during my study, 1953-56 A.C.

Libraries in Granada:- The Library of the University of Granada is constituted of five sections each attached with their faculties and one general section. The University library is preparing a catalogue of the manuscripts and books printed in the 16th and 17th centuries for which this library is particularly known. The general section of the library also contains the names of the Arabic manuscripts and books preserved in the library of the School of Arabic studies in Granada, which was established in 1933, jointly with Miguel Asin Institute of Arabic Studies at Madrid. The Director of this School of Arabic Studies at Granada in 1955 was Luis Seco de Lucena Paredes. The purpose of this institute is to contribute to the investigation of the Hispano-Muslim Culture and to teach modern Spanish culture to the Muslim students of North Africa. The collection of the library is rich but there are very few Arabic manuscripts worth mentioning.

Libraries in Barcelona:- The Central Library of Barcelona was originally founded to serve the purpose of the Institute of Catalan Study established in 1907. It has 1,676 manuscripts mostly in Catalan, 15,061 maps and engravings, stamps, letters and musical instruments. It is important for the study of history and language of Catalonia. There are other two important libraries, the University Library and Historical Archives of the city known as Municipal Institute of History, Barcelona (founded in 1917). This Institute has a library containing 70,000 books and documents. It has many original historical paintings and graphic documents. It possesses sufficient materials for the reconstruction of the social and economic history of Catalonia specially Barcelona from 1249, when Jaime I introduces the custom of maintaining town registers, onwards.

Libraries in other Spanish Towns:-   The five other important cities of Cordova, Seville, Toledo, Saragossa and Valencia were also visited by the writer of the present paper to see the Muslim remains and to study the documents preserved in the libraries of those towns. They have very few Arabic manuscripts; even the University Library of Seville does not possess a good collection of Arabic manuscripts. There are a few rare Arabic manuscripts in the Cathedral of Toledo, but most of them have already been published.

The Arabic manuscripts preserved in the above-mentioned libraries of Spain contain rich data on the social and cultural history of Muslim Spain. It requires to be sifted, re-arranged and analysed to present a complete picture of that side of Hispano-Arab history. The results of such researches made in Hispano-Muslim culture are often published in *Al-Andalus*, Madrid-Granada, the *Boletin de la Real Academia de Ciencias, Bellas Letras y Nobles Artes de Cordoba,* Cordova, and the *Magazine of the Egyptian Institute*, Madrid.

که سلطان سنجر ما منی بار ... برماند و که دیشتی نمزه
پوشی بر سرِ راه ایستاده بیند سلام کرد و سلطان
چیزی بجوانید سری درجنبانید و بزبان
جواب وی نگفت درویش گفت ای پادشاه
سلام کردن سنت است و جواب کلام دادن
فرض من سنت بجای آوردم تو جزا ازدینِ فرض
کردی سلطان ازروی انصاف و صلابت درِّ
اسلام عنان باز کشید و باعتذار درآمده فرمود
که ای درویش بشکر گذاری مشغول بودم از
جواب تو غافل شدم درویش گفت کراشکر

میکنی

بسم الله الرحمن الرحيم صلى الله على سيدنا محمد

قال الشيخ الإمام العالم أبو عبد الله محمد بن عبد الله بن محمد بن إبراهيم اللواتي الطنجي المعروف بابن بطوطة رحمه الله

الحمد لله الذي ذلل الأرض لعباده ليسلكوا منها سبلاً فجاجاً وجعل محمد بن إبراهيم اللواتي ... وأحمد سبحانه ... وسبل الأعلام الشوامخ ووضع فيها من المنافع ... وشرع توكيد مراده وعرفت النجد والمعروف ... ونفس ... من نور من ... في ثمرات ... وضع أقطار صفوف ... ورجع ... عدد وصنع أحد ... وأكمل عرف جملة الأعلام ... وسكن نفست كالأعلام ... من عهود الفقر وهو سخر فطفى الله على سيدنا ومولانا محمد رسوله الذي أوضح لمومن المحجة ووسع نور ... وبقية ... الله يعلو رجمه لنفس ... وخذها خادماً للنفس ... ومن رحم من رتب نشرين ... حق دخل النشر ودين الله ... معظم ... البركات ونطق بصدق

The *Kitāb Yūsuf Zulakha* of Hamdi, Escurial
Library, Ms. no. 1715, fol. 24.

The Kitāb Akriyāt al-Sufūn of Abi'l Qasem Khalaf b. Fanas (dated 23 *Rajab*, 724 June, 1324)

1 For the detailed study of the subject see the works of Abū Bakr ıbn Khayr (Bibliotheca arabico-hispana edition) and Ribera, *Disertaciones*, I,pp. 188-217.

2 Ibn al-Abbār, *Tukmilah* (ed. Codera), no. 7, p. 8.

3 Ribera, *Disertaciones y Opusculos*, I, Madrid, 1928, p. 188.

4 Al-Faraḍī, *The Kitāb Tārikh-i-'Ulamā al Andalus*, no. 774, p. 125.

5 *Ibid.*, I, no. 889, pp. 249-50.

6 Al-Faraḍī, I, no. 1132, np. 316-7.

7 Al-Maqqarī, *Analectes*, I, Leyden, 1855-61, p. 493,

8 Al-Faraḍī, I, no 1150, p. 323,

9 Al-Faraḍī, I, no. 199, p. 58.

10 *Ibid.*, I, no. 281, pp. 81-83; al-Dabbi, *Bughvat al-Multamis*, p. 16; Ibn 'Idhar p. 112; Maqqari, *Analectes*, I, 81; Ribera, *Disertaciones*, I, p. 189.

11 Al-Faraḍī, I, no. 653, p. 181.

12 *Ibid.*, I, no. 268, p. 78; Ribera, *Disertaciones*, I, p. 188.

13 Lopez, *Contribuciones*, p. 91.

14 Al-Faraḍī, I, no. 201, pp. 58-59.

15 *Ibid.*, I, no. 184, p. 53.

16 *Ibid.*, I, no. 1197, p. 336.

17 Ibn al-Khaṭīb, *Ihāṭah*, ms. no. 111 of the Royal Academy of History, Madrid, fol. 135 quoted by Ribera, *Disertaciones*, I, p. 189.

18 Al-Faraḍī, II, no. 1534, p. 38.

19 *Ibid.*, II, no. 1482, p. 26.

20 Al-Faraḍī, II, no. 1528, pp. 31-2.

21 Ibn al-Abbār, *Tukmilah*, no. 86, pp. 31-2.

22 Al-Dabbī, no. 271; Ib.ı al-Faraḍī, no. 1287.

23 Cf. S. M. Imamuddin, *Sobre el Autor de la Cronica Anonima de 'Abd al-Raḥmān III al-Nāṣir* in *Al-Andalus*, XI, 1956, pp. 210-11.

24 Cf. Maqqarī, *Nafḥ al-Ṭib*, II, p. 169; Ibn al Qūṭiyah, *Iftitaḥ al-Andalus*, p. 36.

25 Ibn al-Qūṭiyah, p. 34.

26 *Ibid.*, p. 35.

27 *Ibid.*, p. 35.

28 *Ibid.*, p. 44.

29 Ibn Athir, vol. VI, p. 102; *The Majmū'ah Akhbār Andalus*, pp. 32, 34.

30 *Ibid.*, VI, p. 268; Maqqarī, *Nafḥ al-Ṭib*, I, p. 59.

31 Levi-Provencal, *La civilizacion en Espana*, Argentine, 1953, pp. 64, 85.

32 Abū 'Abd Allāh al-Saqabi a renowned physician of Cordova knew Greek. Cf. Leclerc, *Histoir de la Medicine Arabe*, tomo, I, p. 419; *Disertaciones*, I, p. 191.

33 Al-Faraḍī, I, no. 1290, p. 364.

34 Ibn Abbār, *Tukmilah*, I, no. 362, pp. 106-7; al-Dabbī, no. 94.

35 Gayangos, II, 169; Dozy, *Spanish Islam*, p. 454.

36 Al-Faraḍī, I, no. 884, p. 247.

37 Ibn Abbār, *Tukmilah*, I, no. 284, p. 86; Maqqarī, *Analectes*, II, p. 76.

38 Ribera, *Disertaciones*, I, p. 192.

39 Ibn Bashkuwāl, *Kitab al-Silah*, II, no. 1413, p. 630.

40 *Ibid.*, II, no. 1433, p. 633-4; Ibn Abbār, *Tukmilah*, I, no. 234, p. 71.

41 Maqqari, *Analectes*, I, po. 240, 256; Ribera, *Disertaciones*, I, p. 193.

42 Ibn Abbār, *al-Hullah al-Siyar* (ed. Dozy), p. 101; Gayangos, *The Muhammadan Dynasties in Spain*, I, Appendix, p. XL.

43 Published in twenty one vols. and index Cf. Hitti, *History of the Arabs*, London, 1954, p. 404.

44 Cf. S. M. Imamuddin, *Sohrces of the Economic History of Spain under the Umayyads* (711-1031 A.C.) in *Journal of the Pakistan Historical Society*, Karachi, 1958, pp. 177-8.

45 Maqqarī, *Analectes*, I, p. 605.

46 Al-Farraḍī, I, no. 1398, p. 404.

47 Ibn Bashkuwal, II, no. 1253, p. 563.

48 Al-Dabbi, no. 331.

49 Maqqari, *Analectes*, II, p. 112.

50 Al-Dabbi, no. 883.

51 Al-Faraḍī, II, nos. 1464, 1634, pp. 15-16, 69-70; Ibn Bashkuwal, I, no. 796 p. 367; Ibn Abbār, *Tukmilah*, I, no. 328, pp. 97-8; Al-Dabbi, no. 541; Ribera, *Disertaciones*, I, p. 195.

52 Cf. *Hesperis*, XVIII, 1934, pp. 198-200; Levi-Provencal, *La Civilizacion*, p. 87 n 21.

53 The royal library of Egypt contained during the time of a-lAziz (d. 996 A.C.) only 200,000 books half of that of the library of Cordova. Cf. Maqrizi, I, pp. 408. The royal library of the Abbasids is said to have contained valuable collections but the figure is not known. The library of Mustansiriyah college contained 80,000 books in 1232 A.C.

54 Cf. Ribera, *Disertaciones*, I, pp. 194-5.

55 Ibn Bashkuwāl, I, no. 536, pp. 235-6; al-Dabbi, no. 852.

56 Ibn Abbār, *Tukmilah*, I, no. 417, p. 119.

57 Maqqarī, *Analectes*, I, 136.

58 Cf. Levi-Provencal, *La Civilizacion*, p. 88n22.

59 *Spanish Islam*, p. 558.
  Gayangos, I, pp. XL-XLI.

60 Ibn Bashkuwai in the Appendix of al.

61 Ibn Bashkuwāl, I, no. 679, pp. 303-7.

62 Ibn Abbār, *Tukmilah*, no. 427, p. 122.

63 Maqqari, *Analectes*, II, p. 57.

64 Al-Faraḍī, I, no. 1070, p. 299.

65 Ribera, *Disertaciones*, I, 206.

66 Ibn Bashkuwāl, I, no. 553, pp. 242-4.

67 Al-Faraḍī, II, no. 1597, pp. 58-9.

68 Ibn Abbâr, *Tukmilah*, no. 312, pp. 93-4; Cf. Ribera, *Disertaciones*, I, p. 197.
69 Ibn Bashkuwâl, II, no. 1314, pp. 589-90.
70 *Ibid.*, 1724 (Appendix of al-Faraḍî, II), p. 104.
71 *Ibid.*, II, no. 1144, p. 514.
72 *Ibid.*, I, no. 294, p. 131
73 *Ibid.*, I, no. 508, pp. 223-4.
74 *Bibliutheca arabico-hispana escurialensis*, II, p. 71.
75 Ribera, *Disertaciones*, I, p. 198.
76 Ibn Bashkuwâl, II, no. 1412, p.6 30; Cf. *The Cambridge Medieval History* III, 435.

77 Ibn Bashkuwâl, II, no. 1417, pp. 631-2.
73 *Ibid.*, II, no. 1415, p. 631.
79 Marrâkushi, *al-Mu'jib*, pp. 35-6 text/270 tr. quoted by Levi-Provençal, *L'Espagne*, p. 234; ibn Fayyâḍ, *Cronica de la ciudad de Cordova*, quoted by Ribera, *Disertaciones*, p. 199.
80 Al-Maqqari, *Analectes*, II, p. 631.
81 Munk, *Melanges de philosophie iuive et arabe*, p. 480.
82 Iḥâṭah, I, fol. 131 quoted by Ribera. *Desertaciones*, I, p. 202.

83 Gayangos, II, p. 169.
84 Maqqari, I, 302; Levi-Provençal, *L'Espagne*, p. 234; Albornoz, I, 327.
85 Mâqdisî, p. 239.
86 Ribera, *Disertaciones*, I, p. 204; Albornoz, *La Espana*, I, p. 327.
87 Ibn Abbâr, *Tukmilah*, I, no. 364, p. 108.
88 Maqqari, *Analectes*, I, 641.
89 *Ibid.*, I, 641.

90 Gayangos, I, Appendix, p. XLII.
91 'Ibn al-Qûṭiyah, *Historia de la conquistna de Espana*, p. 170.
92 Ibn Abbâr, *Tukmilah*, no. 1331, p. 462-3.
93 *Ibid.*, no. 1634, p. 583.
94 Al-Maqqari, p. 487.
95 Ibn Bashkuwâl in the Appendix of al-Faraḍî, II, no. 1730, pp. 106-7.
96 Al-Ḍabbî, no. 179.
97 Ibn Abbâr, *Tukmilah*, I, no. 780, pp. 240-2.
98 *Ibid.*, II, no. 1626, pp. 580-1 quoted by Ribera, *Disertaciones*, I, p. 290.
99 Ibn Abbâr, *Tukmilah*, I, no. 734, pp. 216-7.
100 Ibn Bashkuwâl, I, no. 35. pp. 21-3.
101 *Ibid.*, II, no. 1157, pp. 520-21.
102 *Ibid.*, II, no. 1016, p. 464.
103 *Ibid.*, I, no. 443, p. 198.

104 Ibn Bashkuwâl, no. 701, pp. 323-4.
105 *Ibid.*, I, no. 351, pp. 158-60.
106 *Ibid.*, II, no. 1311, p. 588.
107 *Glosario de Simonet*, p. CXLVI.
108 Ibn Abbâr, *Tukmilah*, II, no. 1311, p. 456.
109 Ribera, *Disertaciones*, I, p. 213.
110 Ibn Abbâr, *Tukmilah*, I, no. 902, p. 294.
111 Ribera, *Disertaciones*, I, p. 213.
112 Ibn Abbâr, I, no. 677, p. 199.
113 Ibn Bashkuwâl, I, no. 629, pp. 283, al-Ḍabbi, no. 920.
114 Ibn Abbâr, II, no. 1858, pp. 666-7 quoted by Ribera, *Disertaciones*, I, 214.
115 *Ibid.*, II, no. 1512, p. 538.
116 Ibn Abbâr, I, no. 746, pp. 233-6; Maqqari, *Analectes*, I, p. 607, al-Ḍabbi, no. 778.
117 Iḥâṭah, I, fol. 41v quoted by Ribera, *Disertaciones*, I, p. 215.

118 Ibn Abbâr, I, no. 750, pp. 227-9.
119 Maqqari, *Analectes*, II, p. 359; Ibn Khaṭîb, I, fol. 67 quoted by Ribera, *Disertaciones*, I, pp. 209-210.
110 Maqqari, I, p. 817.
111 Ibn Abbâr, *Tukmilah*, I, no. 1137, pp. 395-6.
112 *Ibid*, II, no. 1192, p. 416.
113 Iḥâṭah, II, fol. 167v, I, fol. 36v quoted by Ribera, *Disertaciones*. I.
114 Iḥâṭah, II, fol. 157v quoted by Ribera, *Disertaciones*, I, p. 217.
115 Ibn Abbâr, I, no. 768, pp. 234-5.
116 Iḥâṭah, III, fol. 141v quoted by Ribera, *Disertaciones*, I, p. 211.
117 P. Lerchundi, *Chrestomatia*, p. 128 quoted by Ribera, *Disertaciones*, I, p. 210.
118 *Ibid*, II, fol. 110 quoted by Ribera, *Desertaciones*, I, p. 211.
119 Ribera, *Desertaciones*, I, p. 216.
120 Iḥâṭah, III, fol. 137r; quoted by Ribera, I, 217.
121 Iḥâṭah, II, fol. 146r; *Jadhwat*, p. 176r quoted Ribera, *Disertaciones*, I, p. 217.

122 Iḥâṭah, I, 34r quoted by Ribera, *Disertaciones*, I, 217.
123 *Ibid.*, III, fol. 99v quoted by Ribera, I, 217.
124 *Ibid.*, fol. 139v quoted by Ribera, I, 216.
125 Iḥâṭah, II, 141v quoted by Ribera, *Disertaciones*, I, 217.
126 Some of the main terms of capitulation were:—
   (a) the Muslim would be guaranteed security of life and property and would be allowed religious freedom;
   (b) they would retain their manners, usages, customs, language and dress;
   (c) the cases between the Muslims and Christians would be heard by mixed tribunals;
   (d) the Muslims would pay only those taxes which they paid to the Muslim kings;
   (e) the neo-Muslims would not be reconverted to their former faith and the Muslims eager to accept Christianity would be given time to think over again and declare their final decision before a Muslim and a Christian judge.

127 Cf. S. M. Imamuddin, *The Influence of Spanish Muslim Civilisation in Islamic Literature*, Lahore, 1956, pp. 357-8.

128 *A Literary History of the Arabs*, London, 1907, p. 435; Cf. S.M. Imamuddin *Sources of the Muslim History of Spain* in the *Journal of Pakistan Historical Society*, Karachi, I, 1953, p. 358.

129 Ribera. *Disertaciones*, I, p. 183.

130 *Rebelion de los Moriscos*, p. 104 quoted by Gayangos, I, p. VIII n. 21.

131 *El Cardenal Ximenes de Cisneros y los manuscritos Arbigo-granadinos* quoted by Ribera, *Disertaciones*, I, p. 183, 227.

132. Ribera, *Disertaciones*, I, p. 183.

133 Ibn al-Faraḍi, I, no. 776, pp. 215-6.

134 *Ibid.*, I, no. 260, p. 76.

135 Ibn Abbār, *Tukmilah*, II, no. 1435, pp. 506-9.

136 Ibn Bashkuwāl, II, no. 960, pp. 439-442; Al-Ḍabbi, no. 1260

137 Maqqari, *Analectes*, I, p. 535.

138 *Ibid.*, I, 499; Ibn Abbār, *Tukmilah*, I, no. 736, pp. 218-9.

139 Marrakushi. p. 261.

140 Ibn al-Faraḍi, II, no. 1647, p. 72.

141 Ibn Abbār, *Tukmilah*, II, no. 2137, pp. 751-2.

142. *Ibid.*, nos. 1, 62, 1930, pp. 590, 689-90.

143 Cf. Ribera, *Disertaciones*, I, p. 219.

144 Ribera, *Disertaciones*, I, 220; Hitty, *History of the Arabs*, p. 521.

145 Ibn al-Faraḍi, I, no. 417, pp. 120-121.

146 Ibn 'Idhārī, II, 315.

147 P. Lerchundi, *Crestomatia*, pp. 93-4; Ribera, *Disertaciones*, I, p. 223.

148 Cf. Ibn Abbār, *Tukmilah*, II, no. 1603, pp. 566-7; Marrakushi, pp. 170-2.

149 Marrakushi. p. 201.

150 Ibn Abbār, *Tukmilah*, I, no. 870, pp. 276-81.

151 Marrakushi, p. 225.

152. Marrakushi, pp. 170-2.

153 Ihāṭah, I, fol. 32v quoted by Ribera, *Disertaciones*, I, p. 224.

154 Ribera, *Disertaciones*, I, p. 225.

155 Janer, *Condicion social de los Moriscos en Espana*, p. 86.

156 Ribera, *Disertaciones*, I, p. 228.

157 *Ibid.*, I, 226.

158 Ribera, *Disertaciones*, I, p. 220.

159 Beaumier, *Rudh al-Cartas* (Sp. tr.), p. 525; Ibn Khaldūn, *Historia Universa*, VII, p. 210.

160 A section of the people is of the opinion that these Arabic manuscripts had been sent by the ruler of Morocco to his son imprisoned in Spain.

161 *La Real Biblioteca de El Escorial* (Discursos en la recepcion del pr. Guillermo Antolin y Parajas Escorial, 1921, pp. 60-61.

162. Ribera, *Disertacoines*, I, pp. 226-227.

163 Simancas, Estado-Legajo, 2644; *Revista de Archivas*, VII, 220, quoted in *Discursos*, pp. 61-62: Jose Quevedo, *Historia Descripcion del Escorial*, Madrid, 1854, p. 105.

164 Cf. L. Lacayoy Santamaria in *Antiguos manuscritos . . . del Monasterio de San Lorenzo del Escorial*, Sevilla, 1878, quoted in *Discursos*, pp. 62-3, Jose Quevedo, pp. 105-106.

165 Simancas, *Secretaria de Estado, Legajo* 1671, p. 2671, quoted in *La Real Biblioteca de El Escorial* (Discursos) Escorial, 1921, p. 640 Jose Quevedo, p. 105.

166 Fiderico Torres, *Nueva Guia de El Escorial*, Madrid, 1952, p. 140.

167 Cf. Dr. S.M. Imamuddin, *Sources of Economic History of Spain under the Umayyads* in *Journal of the Pakistan Historical Society*, vol. VI, Karachi, 1958, pp. 190-191.

168 Cf. *Guia del Lector en la Biblioteca Necional*, Madrid, 1949, pp.90-91

169 The writer of the paper was invited to the opening ceremony of the exhibition. For the details of the exhibition see *Las exposiciones Viejeres* by Justo Garcia Morales Francisco Esteve Barba, Madrid, 1955, pp. 1-49.

170 Cf. Dr. S. M. Imamuddin, *op. cit.*, in the *op. cit.*, VI, Karachi, 1958, pp. 187, 191-192.

171 Imāmuddin, *op. cit.*, in the *op. cit.*, VI, Karachi, 1959, pp. 107, 191—2.17

172. A unique manuscript of *sixteen risalahs* dealing with various social and religious duties of the Muslims written by Ibn Ḥazm is preserved in the library of the Fatih mosque at Constantinople cf. M. Asin Palacios, *Un Codice Inexplorado del Cordobes Ibn Hazm in Al-Andalus*, II, 1934, pp. 1-56.

173 Cf. J.P.H.S., VI, Karachi, 1958, p. 189.

174 *Ibid.*, pp. 189-190.

175 *Ibid.*, p. 188.

176 In connection with his research work on the *Economic History of Muslim Spain under the Umayyads* (711-1031 A.C.) the writer stayed in Spain from the Oct., 1953, to May, 1956, and visited Medieval Muslim towns in Spain and Tetuan and Tangier in North Africa. The Spanish Thesis and its revised English version are ready for press